SIX
MONTHS
& SIX
DAYS

SIX
MONTHS
& SIX
DAYS

MY STRUGGLES DURING THE BANGLADESH WAR OF LIBERATION - A MEMOIR

Amalendu Chatterjee, Ph.D.

ARCHWAY
PUBLISHING

Archway Publishing books may be ordered through booksellers or by contacting:

Archway Publishing
1663 Liberty Drive
Bloomington, IN 47403
www.archwaypublishing.com
844-669-3957

ISBN: 978-1-6657-3863-7 (sc)
ISBN: 978-1-6657-3862-0 (hc)
ISBN: 978-1-6657-4096-8 (e)

Library of Congress Control Number: 2023905551

Print information available on the last page.

Archway Publishing rev. date: 06/02/2023

Acknowledgement

Writing of the book was possible with the encouragement and support from my doctor wife, Arundhati Chatterjee and the constructive editing help from our wonderful doctor sons, Avik Chatterjee, and Ayan Chatterjee.

A Country is not a mere territory; the territory is
only its foundation. The Country is
the idea which rises upon
that foundation: it is the sentiment of love, the sense of
fellowship which binds together all
the sons of that territory.
—Giuseppe Mazzini

Yes, Indian independence or freedom from British colonialism is a cause to celebrate. But seventy-five years of partition into Pakistan and India cannot be a celebration. It is a day of remembering human tragedy and killings, family separation, and hatred between Hindus and Muslims. Ironically, such a day reminds me of another fifty years of a genocide orchestrated by Pakistan for another separation—this one into Pakistan and Bangladesh—and a repeat of this same human tragedy. Once again, the results included killings, family separation, and hatred between Hindus and Muslims. The time is ripe for a history lesson now, so as to avoid spiraling into further separations. It is time for the hope that all human and political conflicts can be resolved without weapons—but, rather, through the art of compromise.

—Amalendu Chatterjee, PhD

Contents

Part III

Part IV

Part V

Preface

While recapping my life story, like other thinkers, I thought much about what I could've done differently? I'm content with what I have personally achieved, and I know my success came at the cost of defying my parents, but they were happy at the end. As for the country I was born in, Bangladesh called East Pakistan during the time this story was taking place, I have many regrets and sorrows. Perhaps the worst was the assassination of our freedom fighting leader while the perpetrators walked free. I escaped the country, and one could call me selfish. But eventually to my greatest satisfaction, I and my family had done my fair share of struggles for the freedom.

While writing this book, I was constantly facing my inner critics: Who are you tell a story and who would care to read your story? Ultimately, however, it wasn't even that I had the moral authority of telling at least my own story as I wished but the pure human tragedies that I witnessed compelled me to do so.

This is a history written by one individual on behalf of millions who didn't have the chance to live to tell the story or are not as privileged as me to write it. Million Hindus migrated to India due to oppressive rules and regulations orchestrated by the Pakistani military since 1947. In contrast, not so many Muslims from India migrated to Pakistan though Pakistan was created for Muslims only leaving more than its own population in India. Because India had a different vision of secularism and democracy – a country for all. Yes, there were many race-related events in India, but all were reactionary and there had never been documented government policies or regulations in support of that. There had never been a consistent and systematic story of the Bangladesh revolution and its aftermath events. Lately, Bangladesh has been using the same playbook Pakistan used against its minorities – brain washing two or three generations of Bangladeshi Muslims against Hindus and India. A depressing tale with the latest look of the society must be told for general awareness and that has been my attempt in the book.

I was just an unknown kid from an island with a big dream and vision with little knowledge of political and social maneuver. I was a kid with analytical mind. I was a kid with full of curiosities. I was a kid with fairness to all as guided by my father doctor. I was a kid well liked in the island, college, and professional life. I was a technocrat with a vision that helped me to write many technical articles including a book, 'Autonomous and Integrated Parking and Transportation Services'.

I was also proud when I saw the President Biden's approved infrastructure bill addressed many ideas of the book for a visionary transportation system. I was also behind the implementation of the first North Carolina information Superhighway for distance learning and telemedicine in 1990. The infrastructure of such broadband network connected the whole world during Covid crisis to go virtual for all daily life including education, connecting friends, and running business. It was fulfilling to think where we had been without such worldwide interconnection in the 21st century during covid epidemic when all businesses including education were conducted by Zoom. I was also active in children sports club – Raleigh Swimming Association (RSA). I was a board member of Rosemont Homeowners Association (HOA). I retired in 2017 and became active in politics. I was appointed board member twice by the North Carolina Governor, Mr. Cooper, the board of science, technology, and Innovation (BSTI); and the board of agriculture finance authority (NCAFA). I came to know many state as well as federal USA politicians. Politics, though not always fair, are very important for an influence of your thought in the policy implementation. Figure below shows author's picture with then senator Biden and North Carolins Secretary of State, Elaine Marshall who was running for the US senate in 2014.

As for the second or third question, any democratic minded person with the central theme of democracy, 'The Majority Rules with the Full Protection of the Minority Right' can get some idea to save the human tragedy. I know it is easier said than done at least for a heterogeneous country like Bangladesh where ethnicity, and religions with the mix of politics play a dominant role. For a homogeneous country like Japan or Vietnam democratic principles are easier to implement with less polarization. But for Bangladesh, it is complex because it is an Islamic country with many other ethnicities. The incident regarding my family and sacrifice of so many in 1971 and later in 1975 to 2008 should touch the heart of many to rethink how Bangladesh could be a model Islamic but democratic country. Some may say it may be lost case, but I never gave up hope. Democratic minded people of the world who want to make a difference may read the book to explore the following:

- Why is a full restoration of the 1972 Bangladesh secular constitution required?
- Creating an opportunity of an ideal model democratic country in an Islamic society.

- Banning all religious political parties to avoid sociopolitical polarization and unnecessary tension.
- Transformation of religious madrasas into schools of science and math.
- Foundation of Hindu, Buddhist, and Christian communities through legislation for fairness.
- Formation of one cabinet level minister positions for minority.
- Proportional representation of minorities in the parliament.
- Holding Pakistan and its 90,000 soldiers accountable who engaged in mass killings of religious minorities.
- Welfare of million Bangladeshis who are still looking for escape due to lack of socio-political justice.

Independence of a country cannot be a cause of celebration unless its people are free of discrimination. At 50 years of independent Bangladesh minorities still feel the emotion of killing, family separation and Hindu-Muslim hates.

Part I

Chapter 1

Beginning The Story

Pakistan was a byproduct of a single concept, Islam (or Muslim), with no consideration of other human factors, such as ethnic and cultural compositions. Pakistan was a state proud of religion, a quasi-theocracy. Religion aside, the new country was indifferent to a major linguistic reality. The people of East Pakistan spoke Bengali, which had little to do with Urdu.

East Pakistan, now Bangladesh, was part of Pakistan because over 60 percent of its population were Muslims, and close to 40 percent were other ethnic minorities, including Hindus. Besides religion, there were many fundamental differences between East and West Pakistan. Bangladesh after the liberation, had evolved quickly to be a complicated country beyond what the founding father, Sheikh Mujibur Rahman, dreamed. Pakistan was a country partitioned by the British to please the Muslim League (ML) leaders. ML's struggle or effort compared to the Indian Congress party's "Quit India" movement was minimum. For Bangladesh, struggle was much harder.

In 1971, I had to take a reactive but quick decision to save my life at the Kaptai hydroelectric dam far away from the island where I was born. I had to leave Kaptai and the job after observing a human massacre. Bengali-speaking Muslim employees were killing Urdu-speaking non-Bengalis, or Biharis, who were accused of being military cooperators before the military appeared at Kaptai. I rationalized my spontaneous decision with simple reason—my family and the opposition to the military crackdown on innocent citizens, especially minorities. There had been military crackdowns before, but the one in 1971 was unreal, as it came in the middle of negotiation for handing over the power to the elected majority, which the public perceived.

A democratic election in 1969 gave a landslide victory to the Awami League (AL) party from East Pakistan, but West Pakistanis defied all election results for the sake of holding power. The Nixon-Kissinger administration had vested interests and orchestrated a sophisticated plan to help Pakistan. Mr. Zulfikar Ali Bhutto, the leader of Pakistan People's Party (PPP), also played a significant role in the negotiation, though he lost the election. His claim was that he held majority votes in West Pakistan. In hindsight, my participation in the civil war had a much wider implication, as many things were slowly revealed during and after the initial success. I did not know the conspiracies that brewed in Pakistan's military administration then, though I know now. I regret that I knew very little of the country I was supposed to love. My parents were also blindfolded by an affection for the country.

Unfortunately, the proper history of Pakistan's political doctrine and philosophy was never taught. I wish the military administration knew the significance of learning history as explained by Marilyn vos Savant of the *Parade Magazine* on September 11, 2022:

> The chronicle of historical events teaches us—bit by bit by bit—about civilization, human nature, and its consequences. Imagine two men after a centuries-long journey in time. One was asleep all day; the other was awake. The latter witnessed every triumph and calamity, learned where beauty flowered and where it died, watched the greatest and most inglorious fights of good against evil. Which would you choose as a leader? As a friend? Which would you rather be, the man who saw everything or the man who saw nothing? Your answer shows why you should study history.

The education system was more aligned with the religious philosophy. It was advantageous to the military administration to establish more mosques than schools for girls. I could simply leave the country at the beginning of the crackdown when I had an opportunity to become a refugee in India. In that case, I would have been in a safer place. I could have missed all the challenges and life-and-death experiences in the successful civil war. That, by itself, had enough material for my memoir. New information about the war since 1972 adds a different dimension to the book. An overview of Pakistan's complicated past and events leading to the freedom movement of 1971 would add a better foundation, revealing many secrets of wrongdoings by Muslim League leaders from the beginning. It would also start a different narrative because of the assassination of Bangladesh's Founding Father. The honeymoon was short-lived. The saddest part was a manipulation of Bangladesh's founding progressive constitution to a nonsecular and Islamic constitution.

Chapter 2

Glamourous Engineering Profession

My engineering job and my first posting in Barisal, a district headquarter in East Pakistan, had many perks and rewards. Exposers to the public outside the office was also glamorous. Finishing the student life and getting a good paying job as an engineer were all gratifying. It would have been more gratifying if I did not have a stigma of being a minority. After the turbulent student life, I thought, I would start a peaceful life in a remote corner of the country. But alas, that never happened.

It was a welcoming event when I arrived in my office at Barisal. My parents also visited me a few months after I joined. They were overwhelmed with all arrangements of my stay—free quarters, a pickup truck with a driver, a speed boat, and so on. My parents took the opportunity to talk to my friends about convincing me to get married. That I was not entertaining their proposal was heartbreaking for them. Of course, my friends lured me into being introduced to several families with prospective brides. Having a family could have been a nightmare during the civil war. I am glad I had a strong will to keep my promise of pursuing my dream of going abroad. Strong will was the culmination of my feeling from childhood that to remain a minority in an Islamic country would be a curse.

Barisal had a small power station, so the workload was not heavy. A recreational club established by the British was very entertaining. Barisal had once been a river port transporting goods from different islands to Dhaka or Chittagong. I became a member of the club and developed social skills, such as playing tennis, squash, and drinking.

Those activities helped me in two ways: (1) I got friendly with other officers in the district who were helpful in the job of establishing the right of way (easement of the power line), and (2) they were a good use of my time during weekends and holidays.

I was given the charge of supervising the construction of the thirty to forty miles of 132-kV transmission lines. The project was approved to appease an Islamic cleric (Sharshina Pir) who was a friend of President Ayub Khan. It was a pet project of President Ayub Khan to please a religious but powerful individual. Mr. Ayub Khan even visited the place several times to raise his profile in the community during the early stage of the project. Electricity to a holy place of worships with no industrial base was hard to economically justify. Design, planning and even survey of the route had been completed by foreign companies—Czechoslovakian and Japanese. A Czechoslovakian consultant did the design, and a Japanese contractor supplied the materials. My job was supervising the work of the contractor—putting in foundation of the tower and erecting the electric power lines with proper insulation as per specification of the designer. To make some economic sense of the project, I even planned some power substations for electricity usage by a few schools and colleges on the route. Unfortunately, the practical aspect of the job was to handle many unforeseen issues of the social reality never taught in the engineering class.

Behind all those glamours, there were many unofficial opportunities for vested individuals to make quick money —bribes. Sometimes, the choices made by higher officials were forced on you. The hierarchy of the Water and Power Development Authority (WAPDA) at a construction site like the Barisal power line consisted of chief engineer, who approved the construction bid of large contracts, especially those sponsored by foreign aid and superintendent engineer, who collected bids and recommended the contractor for approval by the chief engineer. All those logistics were completed prior to the executive engineer being entrusted with the completion of the project at the site. Junior engineers or site engineers like me were charged with the quality and quantity of work in progress. The site engineer had a tool called a measurement book (MB) to recommend payments. The executive engineer approved the payment, and the accountant wrote the check.

The workflow process became a chain filled with links of corruption. Everybody in the link had a de facto demand or quota (a percentage) on the total approved payment to the contractor. Anybody breaking the link, meaning not accepting the bribe percentage, could create a problem for the contractor. I became a victim of such link and paid the price for it. I was transferred to the Kaptai Academy. It started with the chief engineer when he awarded the contract. The superintendent engineer got a cut when he recommended the contractor to the chief engineer for the award and so on. All these were my learning experience, as was the time a contractor approached me with a bundle of cash in an envelope in exchange for compromising the quality of work with cheaper stone than specified for the foundation of the power towers.

The sections that follow describe two other instances of corrupt environments.

Unwritten Instance of Discrimination

My routine job was to visit the site frequently to check the progress and the quality of work. While visiting the site the first time, I noticed one odd engineering surprise. The line of sight of the power line was crooked. Such power line route was generally supposed to be as straight as possible. After investigation, it was revealed that local Muslim influence had caused the line to be rerouted over minority properties. For power lines, a fifty-foot clearance, called a "right-of-way," was required on both sides.

Such easement or right-of-way meant displacement of houses, cutting trees, and clearing other permanent installations. Residents were not happy to give away their property rights. There was incentive of compensation available for the right-of-way, of course. There were problems facing the officer in charge, who had to calculate the right compensation amount. Market values were much higher than the official rate. First, the rate set by the British rule, maybe more than a hundred years back, was too low. Residents could earn their yearly livelihood by selling produce from their few coconut and mango trees at the current market rate, which were much higher than the compensation for the tree itself. Second, I could inflate units to increase the compensation amount, but doing so is subject to legal liability. I had to go out of the way to make residents satisfied with less resistance.

I came up with one innovative way to resolve the dilemma—increase the number of units of everything and use bulldozers immediately to clear the right of way. Bull dodgers were helpful to erase evidence in case of disputes. This was done after a negotiated number was reached for the owner's satisfactory compensation. Some minorities were happy to get the money through the government channel and then leave the country with no hustle or harassment by neighbors. For some other minorities, it was almost like losing their permanent livelihood. Some could neither fight the court nor leave the country. They knew the court would always be biased.

Shocking Instance Of Bribe

I was fresh out of college with a naive philosophy about a pure world. Soon, I found out the reality at the engineering site was different. I had absolute authority over the work of the contractor for payments. That kind of power also leads to an opening of corruption. Both the volume of work and the quality of work were under my control. To maintain such standard, I had to make many surprise visits. This was not to the contractor's liking, of course. The contractor was very friendly and cooperative at the beginning. He was willing to do many personal favors in exchange for making extraordinary profits. That drew my suspicion.

For power lines, the foundation of the towers is extremely critical, especially on marshy land across many river crossings. Sinkholes or sand boiling were very common. Raw materials such as cement, sand, steel, and gravel used for the foundation had to be of high quality. During one of my surprise visits, I saw a heap of brick chips, instead of stone chips as per spec, lying around the foundation. I stopped the work on the foundation and asked the contractor's officer in charge to replace the brick chips with stone chips. That did not go well with the contractor's bottom line. His argument was in favor of keeping the work schedule without delay and keeping the cost down.

My engineering guts told me I could not sacrifice the quality of the foundation to keep the schedule. It was a case of liabilities and fear in case the tower would fall. One incident like this would jeopardize my whole engineering professional life.

The next morning, the contractor knocked at my office and left quickly with an envelope. My belief was it could be a letter about correcting the quality by the contractor. Instead, the envelope was very thick—stuffed with of high-value currency notes. I complained to the higher authority. I was told to make a mini sample of the foundation using materials at the site and then send it for the strength test by the Dhaka research lab. That test result never came back despite repeated reminders. Later, I found out that the contractor was a close friend of the minister in charge. The contractor was a Muslim League supporter and had a direct line to the power minister. I saw no chance of getting any support from my superiors.

The episode convinced me to ask for a transfer from the field job to an academic setting. In fact, the same contractor helped me to take that transfer for his own interest. Kaptai Engineering Academy was an in-service training center. The academy center was free of all site contractors. I thought it would also help me to proceed with my plan for higher studies. I had to change my lifestyle from playing tennis or squash to fishing and hunting along the Karnafuli River and hilly areas of the dam.

Later, I realized the timing of the transfer was not perfect. The country had grievances against the military administration, Ayub Khan, and Yahya Khan. Continuous unrest and protest on the street grew day by day. Such protests became violent as Yahya Khan delayed respecting the mandate by the people in an election approved by him. At the academy, the workload was reasonable, three to four engineering training sessions at different levels in a year. I conducted one such session only, and then everything stopped. The whole East Pakistan administration came to a standstill. Telecommunications, postal systems, and transportation could not operate because people were protesting. In the process, employees did not receive their salaries for months.

In contrast to Barisal, Kaptai was totally different socially, geographically, and demographically, as well as climate wise. Barisal was a marshy land, and Kaptai was a hilly land with dry air. Kaptai had a very scenic landscape. The only dam in Bangladesh was built in 1962 over the Karnafuli River to generate 232 megawatts of electricity—supplying major part of the electricity demand of East Pakistan at that time. The dam was conceived during the British rule but completed by an American company during the Ayub's regime with aid from the United States. The area was mostly populated by local tribes called Chakma with their own language and culture. Slowly, they could speak Bengali. The engineering academy was a separate administrative unit from the dam project. There were close to 350 to 400 employees in the combined operations. Most of the employees were Biharis (immigrant Muslims from Bihar, an Indian province), including the chief engineer. Even I had two Bihari employees. Everyone was hopeful there would be peaceful transfer of power from the army to the civilian government.

Betrayal By The Administration

To our dismay, the dark day of March 25, 1971, was imposed on East Pakistan. The BBC and Akashvani Kolkata (West Bengal radio station) were broadcasting reports of the indiscriminate killing of intellectuals, Hindu professors, and students. Mr. Deb Dulal Bandyopadhyay (a news reader at Akashvani) became a household name in Bangladesh and among freedom fighters. His voice and his way of delivering optimistic news would bring a lifeline to all those who were in trenches and had been suffering from malnutrition and emotional depression. We were all glued to these two stations—the only form of recreation in the evening time.

The hallmark of the Hindu students' residence, Jagannath Hall, was attacked with mortar shells. Hundreds were killed. Big cities were the military's first target. They thought if they could control popular university cities, they would be able to keep Pakistan as it was. The military had this biased view that Hindus, with India's help, were responsible for all the unrest. That was not true initially. Such biased views were reflected in all military policies and field operations. All local radical Islamists were infected by the military with such false propaganda.

Differentiating Terrorism – India Vs USA

The Line Of Control (LOC) demarcation established by the UN became the source of all terrorism. Pakistani terrorists were trained behind the LOC. Many Afghani or other terrorists also joined them for training. All such activities supported by the Pakistani government were revealed after the terrorist attack on US soil, September 11, 2001. Pakistani President Parvez Musharraf made an interesting comment on the issue as well. He told Western reporters terrorism against India and global terrorism defined by the United States of America could not be equated. India was our enemy, and so terrorism against India must be fought differently while cooperating with the United States against global terrorism. President Musharraf was hungry for US dollars, and the United States was desperate to fight global terrorism.[1] There was a match of devils' minds. Practically, Parvez Musharraf played dubious games for US favor—political and financial.

Reviving Ottoman Empire

The mindset of Pakistani leaders was corrupt from the beginning causing its own self-humiliation. Pakistan's dream of the revival of the Ottoman Empire by ML leaders from the early stage of the country was distasteful. Land was more important to ML than the people living in the land. Even today, the military calls the shots, though Pakistan boasts of a democracy. Pakistan failed for many reasons. Three reasons I can cite

---

[1] House Hearing, 114 Congress, from the U.S. Government Publishing Office.

from my childhood experience are (1) the fake dream of building back the Ottoman Empire; (2) not recognizing the well-established and highly respected Bengali language and culture of East Pakistan; and, of course, (3) supporting terrorism against India through Kashmir.

Muslim League leaders were too ambitious and power hungry. They wanted to go back to the nine hundred-year-old Indian history of Islamic rule. A sudden attack on the princely state of Kashmir in 1947, within three months of partition, surprised India. India was busy building a country from scratch for the right secular and progressive democracy for all. There could have been ways to reach a negotiated agreement for peaceful coexistence before the rivalry reached a state of no return. The sudden Kasmir attack by Pakistan did not serve the purpose of the peaceful coexistence of two newly formed countries. Instead, Pakistani radical leaders, with army support, became aggressive in their pursuit of an unrealistic Islamic dream. Pakistan thought capturing Kashmir would be easy. Then they would be able to conquer the rest of India under Muslim rule.

The attempt was foiled. But India, or Prime Minister Nehru made the mistake of going to the United Nations (UN), even against the will of Sheikh Mohammad Abdullah, for dispute resolution. The Kashmiris and the rest of India have been paying the price since then. The UN resolution emboldened Pakistan to keep the rivalry alive forever. It was hope against hope that the Pakistani military would come to its senses at the despair of humanity. The United States fell into Pakistan's misguided trap of Islamism. Nixon-Kissinger's geopolitical interest in linking China with Pakistan to help break the China-Russia axis was another dynamic.

In fact, Bangladesh's civil war started the day Mr. Jinnah, self-declared founding father of Pakistan, unilaterally declared Urdu to be the only state language while attending a political gathering in Dhaka in 1948 with no respect for parliamentarian decision. Student protests started that very day, and then political parties and party leaders over the years worked together to demand a federated East Pakistan with its own language and culture. In addition, the activism by students continued for years, and many students were killed in the process. It reached its climax when then President Ayub Khan charged Awami League (AL) leader Sheikh Mujibur Rahman with a conspiracy to secede[2].

In the end, instead of handing over the power to a democratically elected government, Ayub Khan chose his right-hand man, Yahaya Khan, to take over. Protests continued against President Ayub Khan to Mujib's six-point demand of East Pakistan's complete autonomy with a central federation. In addition, the student bodies of both provinces (East and West Pakistan) had eleven points of demand, including the abolition of the military rule. There was almost a complete government shutdown. Instead, Yahya Khan took over, and started the same military-style rule.

Yahya Khan promised elections in the face of protest and shutdown of government activities. He conspired with Z. A. Bhutto of Pakistan People's Party (PPP) to keep the power after Mujibur Rahman won a landslide victory in the election. And that military usurp of an otherwise democratic election for a civilian government triggered a conflict that resulted in the Bangladesh genocide on March 25, 1971. During the 1971 conflict, United States and Pakistan tried the same tactic. Pakistan had a good relationship with China. The Nixon-Kissinger administration wanted to tap that relationship for their vested international interests. Indira Gandhi outsmarted them with other international allies, without the United States of America. Burning issues related to ten million refugees in India became the bargaining tool for Indira Gandhi's leadership.

Prevailing Sad State of Bangladesh

The current state of affairs in the country are not very promising for minorities. Bangladesh is borrowing from the same playbook Pakistan has used since its inception. It's very sad. Military domination, negligence of proper democracy, manipulation by selfish leaders, religious discrimination, and minority marginalization have established

---

[2] Talbot 1998, p. 190 "The case against them became known as the Agartala Conspiracy Case since it was at Agartala that the accused were alleged to have met Indian army officers"

a platform of polarization and perpetual internal threat against Pakistan's own existence. Such threat destabilized its very existence. In addition, the threat has spilled over neighboring countries due to lack of trust between them.

Now, Bangladesh has fallen into the Pakistani or Islamic trap, spoiling an opportunity for a secular and progressive democracy. Bangladesh maintained cordial terms with India on and off, hampering its progress in many fronts. Seventy-five years after independence, India's economy and world standing in terms of sociopolitical status went up. India also moved forward in large strides, even in the job-scarce economy with a diverse Muslim population. Bangladesh had an opportunity, but it is slipping away slowly. Lately, even without an apology for the 1971 atrocities, Bangladesh has been pursuing a friendly relationship with Pakistan. This is unforgivable, of course, to the minority.

An example of discriminatory behavior toward the minority is reflected in a manifesto presented to the prime minister, Sheikh Hasina, by the coalition of Bangladeshi American Religious and Ethnic Minorities when she was visiting UNO's 77th session in New York. Janmabhumi, a New York based Bangladeshi weekly published a Bengali article on the subject on September 22, 2022

Dramatic First Month

My original intention of going to Sandwip after quitting the office at Kaptai was disrupted due to situations beyond my control. Sandwip was an isolated island located close to the Chittagong naval port and always risky to cross. The Pakistan Army was continuously active to protect the naval port. Public transportation by ship or ferry was not allowed without army permission. Before or after the permission, there would be random checkpoints while boarding the ship or the boat. There was no escape for minorities if caught "red-handed" under such circumstances. There was no way to walk to the island. I was blindly following millions of displaced people from large cities with no fixed destination. I was the only islander. But there were people fleeing from cities to villages, millions crossing to India. Some decided to join the splinter groups on the way to fight the Pakistan Army. All I wanted first was to reunite with my family. I ended up in Barisal while wandering several days from place to place. Support and cooperation, including food and shelter received from unknown villagers, were unprecedented.

In Barisal village, I took a shelter in the house of a distant aunt. I also met many neighbors of my aunt, including many city dwellers who took shelter there. As I stayed there for many days, they became real friends during the crisis. They all became a family, and we stayed together until the military invaded the village. Mr. Subodh Dey was one of my acquaintances from my previous job in Barisal city. He was a lawyer by profession, and I used him for legal advice while clearing the right-of-way for building the power line. It was serendipitous that I met them again in my maternal aunt's house.

The Dey family had a college-going girl, and she started flirting with me. Unfortunately, I did not know what to do, other than saving girls like her from the army torture. That was, of course, another reason for my involvement in initiating humanity work. I did not want to show my affection or weakness as a lesson to others. The Dey family and others, including me, crossed the border together. I even visited the girl's uncle's home a couple of times in Kolkata. I was too busy working for the Bangladeshi government in exile and preparing for my journey to Canada, and so indulgence of romantic affairs was out of question. The girl was the only daughter of Mr. Dey and was beautiful and attractive, maybe twenty-two or twenty-three years old. She graduated from Barisal B. M. College but did not have much ambition. She had a cousin who was not beautiful but overly ambitious. I did not have time to pursue either of them.

Family Love And Survival Anxiety

It took me a while to decide on my next move. I had a firm determination to save lives and free the country from brutal slaughtering. Barisal's villages are always submerged during the summer and rainy seasons. The military used to travel by speedboat, anchoring the boat in a convenient place so they could run away quickly if they saw any danger of counterattack. They would then walk past the paddy field with megaphone and automatic rifles. This chase by the military firmly united the Hindus and the Muslims of Awami League (AL) supporters. We formed a local group. Our mission was not to allow any outsider other than displaced people to penetrate the area. It worked.

During this period, there was a radio broadcast banning all Pakistani high-stake notes surprising all minorities hiding with cash reserve. It was concluded that the objectives of such an announcement were two: 1) cripple the economic backbone of the minorities especially rich Hindus and 2) hunt down minorities when they show up in the bank for bank deposit. I came up with a strategy to counter such heinous act, looking for good Muslim Samaritans in the neighborhood. Details are described further in Chapter 7. After the episode, I concluded there was no time to look back. Thinking of my family kept me moving forward.

When the military attacked the neighborhood, we had to run away empty-handed. In my six months of hiding, we could never enter that house again. Later, I learned the house was ransacked from top to bottom because they knew who (well-to do people) had been taking shelter in the house. Most of them involved in such inhuman activities were Islamists and minority haters. Even after such crisis, some were non-committal on the liberation and some were anti-liberators, hoping a strong coexistence with West Pakistan.

Traumatic Nine Months

Memories of those nine months, first in Bangladesh trenches and then with the Bangladeshi exile government in Kolkata, haunted me all my life in Canada and The United States. For six months, I struggled for my life in the Barisal trenches, and for three months I was at Mujib Nagar, a working place for the Bangladeshi government in exile. Mujib Nagar was a place on Theater Road, Kolkata. After nine months of a tumultuous, hard life, Bangladesh was liberated.

I thought the liberation would end the human tragedy once and for all. But no. In Canada, I was busy with my profession and with raising a family. My spirit and motivation to write a memoir was always there. I became successful at the end of the struggle. I could not forget the traumatic experience of those nine months. But most disturbing was what happened afterwards. Traumatic changes in human attitude were to be recorded for historical reasons. All of it—the high-end elite life of the profession; constant queries about my parents; memories of people left behind, of human tragedy, and of escape from a military bullet that had landed within ten feet of me; Islamization of the country; my father's death; the uprooting of the family; and on and on were bothering me day and night. Recent event after event in Bangladesh, along with the nightmares and emotional scars of those nine months and a feeling of helplessness for the future led my activism in Canada and then in the United States. Though our dream of a visionary democratic country was lost, hope had to be revived—that is the objective of this memoir.

My first job in East Pakistan gave me an opportunity to socialize with other government officials and develop a repertoire. It was very comfortable but short-lived, less than three years (1968-1971). In that juncture of my professional beginning my parents wanted me to get married. That was before liberation.

In contrast, after the liberation, it was a time of constant hugging and kissing after nine months. Those nine months were traumatic for them as well as for me. My whereabouts had been unknown; now, it was as if they'd found a lost child. I could not be away from their sight for a second, and there were questions after questions as to my movements in the jungle and then in the government in exile in India. The stories of human tragedy shocked them. They thought one of them could have befallen me. That thought alone caused tears to spill from their eyes. That alone warned me not to randomly socialize with Muslim neighbors even after the liberation. The spirit of radical Islamization, especially in villages, was still in existence. My presence could trigger it again to harm me or my family.

Those few days with the family were wonderful moments of my life that have kept me going until today. I have my own family now. My parents were very sad to say goodbye to me when I left for my next venture. I was so moved by their love and affection that I wanted to help others who were deprived of what I had at the end; it was the cause of my activism from abroad. My worst nightmares came true when my father got sick in 1978, and I could not visit him due to the revival of Pakistani-like Bengali Islamic regime.

I have long pondered the loss of an opportunity on the part of Bangladesh to be an ideal Islamic but democratic country—an achievement that could be showcased on the world stage. The current prevailing political, social, and economic situation would never allow that lost opportunity to come in my lifetime, unless a leader like Sheikh Mujibur Rahman were to emerge with a vision of equality for all. Success of a revolution is very rare in history and can happen, maybe, once in a century, when a country is totally destabilized—as happened in 1971 for Bangladesh. Otherwise, the minority would have to find their own ways to migrate to India or abroad and put pressure on Bangladesh for a proportional land demand as part of India. Since then, four generations of the Bangladeshi population (from 1947 to 2018) had been brainwashed with an infrastructure of madrasa education, and it would be difficult to turn back from that unfortunate fate.

To summarize, the country went into a freefall due to the rebirth of the autocracy and the whims of few individuals misusing foreign aids. Nobody was innovative and thoughtful enough of real industry and educational infrastructures with their own for sustainability. Millions could not rise above the poverty level. This was afforded to only a few, who were greedy and power hungry and who exploited the new administration in exchange for their own selfish interests even before the country could stand on its own feet.

I learned a lot through the good times as well hard time that guided my life to be successful in the end. It was not easy to come to Canada, and persistent efforts paid off. Now, because I am in a country where personal freedom and hard work are valued, I want to promote the same values back home in gratitude to my parents. My father, on the other hand, did all the right things in an autocratic country with unfair policies and regulations that worked against the minority. That environment denied him of all his personal and democratic rights. His dream was shattered at the end of his life due to national and international politics, religious persecution, and social discrimination. My father did not want to migrate to India to preserve his pride, honor, prestige, assets, and all human aspirations. Alas, all fell apart during and after the Bangladesh liberation movement. You can call it a tragedy perpetrated against one human being by the other because they had different ethnicities. All ray of hopes for the Bangladeshi minority were crushed in a matter of three years.

That was also the time when I was busy building my career and raising my own family with a doctor wife, Arundhati Chatterjee. She was doing her residency with two of our infant children. Finally, I finished my PhD in computer communications (doing research with DARPA-related projects) in 1977. DARPA stands for Defense Advance Research Project Agency. I landed my dream job in the field of telecommunications, Bell Canada. Despite deserving qualifications, Pakistan would not recruit minorities in such lucrative jobs.

Today, I have two wonderful grownup children. Both are medical doctors. While in the United States, in my professional career, I always remembered where I came from and wanted to help people in distress back home. I have worked to raise awareness, nationally and internationally, about what happened to minorities in Bangladesh, to keep the record straight for those who would be writing histories of Bangladesh during the decades I was there. Perhaps that may be a service more valuable than what my father wished me to be—a doctor healing patients. I hope writing my story here may heal a society and a nation, while correcting Bangladesh's real history.

Unfortunately, I had to leave the country within nine months after the liberation. Everybody wanted a quick glory of the movement and instant gratification. Many were awarded, rightfully or wrongfully, with high-ranking jobs, even though they were not qualified. Business ownership was handed over to unexperienced people. Such favoritism was the source of discontent among many Bangladeshi civilians and soldiers. As in Pakistan's history, the Bangladeshi army took an advantage of this situation to grab power by assassinating Mujibur Rahman.

New Government With Chaotic Administration

India's help was essential for the liberation. India was not prudent enough to help Bangladesh to stand on its own after the liberation - sustainability. It was difficult to understand if this oversight was intentional or if India thought nothing could go wrong with such a popular leader as the head of the newly formed country. India did not spend much time attaining a firm grasp of Bangladesh's real needs—a new administrative and business infrastructure. India did not understand the mindset of its Muslim population, which had been brainwashed by the previous military regime over a few decades. India presumed Bangladesh would always be a follower state of India administratively, economically, and politically. Alas, India was deeply wrong!

India was also wrong in allowing Indian businesses to run their course of meeting the essential daily requirements of Bangladesh's people (mainly staple food). Indian businesses thought it would be a captive market for price gauging. Indian businesses tried to take advantage of Bangladeshi political leaders. Sheikh Mujibur Rahman did not have the administrative experience necessary to take the control over the chaotic situation. Everybody had guns to resolve daily disputes in the street. West Pakistani military established all industries in the west using raw materials from the east. Jute and rice industries were examples. Bangladesh depended fully on India for daily needs, and Indian businesses charged whatever they wanted. Bangladeshis were always happy growing staples like rice, vegetables, and so on in the same land. Nine months of war and infighting among people did not help Bangladeshis get their daily meal, as the chaos created a temporary shortage of food.

Chapter 3

Relentless Efforts To Land In Canada

For engineers, going abroad was restricted with one layer of bureaucracy in Pakistan. For minorities, there were many other layers of bureaucratic restrictions because of personal bias or discriminatory laws. One of the commitments I had to make was to come back to serve the country after achieving my foreign degree before permission would be granted to go abroad. My parents had to sign a promissory note separately as well, guaranteeing my return. This was applicable whether a minority student accepted a scholarship or went on his own for higher degrees. Such a process could take months from remote cities because applications were always processed at the foreign ministry office. Several of my attempts, at least three, failed for different reasons. And then came the civil war. Maybe it could have been a blessing in disguise.

I was posted as an engineer at a rural site in Barisal. I preferred a big city like Dhaka. It could have been easier to get updated information on my application as it moved around the bureaucratic layers. I had to bribe the appropriate people at the ministry office for the next step of the process. It was white-collar corruption. I had to take personal time off from Barisal to travel to Dhaka at my own expense many times. There were corruption and bribery at every branch of the government offices. But it was a different kind of corruption than that at the construction site.

The process was a double-edged sword for a minority officer at the construction site. As a minority officer, I had to play it safe all the time. I would be guilty if anything went wrong, bribe or no bribe; I would be guilty if the work was delayed. It was like finger-pointing by someone by default if you were a minority officer. So, I opted for a transfer to Kaptai Academy, an institute for in-service training after three years in Barisal. Kaptai has a dam over Karnafuli River supplying almost half of the electricity requirements for Bangladesh at the time. Many of my Muslim friends had gotten the job of their choice. Many got scholarships to go abroad as well. I wanted a job in the department of telecommunications or Pakistan Civil Service. But I was told not to even apply when asking for recommendations from Muslim professors. My earnest desire to join the telecommunication department was crushed. The telecommunications department had been considered the vital national security infrastructure, and minorities could not be trusted with any job there, though qualified people like me were plenty.

But it did not matter that much, as I was determined to go for a PhD program. There were some struggles to finish an elaborate application process, which required proper and good references from different professors. Professors were not all always available or had left the country for their own career aspirations. I was awarded a few scholarships, but I could not bypass the layers in place to take advantage of any of them.

I then attempted to depend on the benevolence of foreign universities. I was successful in achieving both admission and assistantship at the University of Ottawa. I had to keep my attempts to go abroad secret from my employer to avoid job humiliation. Such secrecy raised the difficulty of getting good recommendations. The admission was extended by the university from one session to the next.

In the middle of the third extension in 1971, the beginning of a national crisis jeopardized my life's plan. Prospects of a doctoral program in Canada became doubtful. Instead, I found myself in the jungle during the civil war in 1971. I was fighting to save the lives of those who had been displaced from the urban and suburban areas to avoid the military atrocities. I had to survive for six months, during which I saved not only my own life but also others' lives from two opposing forces—the military and the Islamists. This lasted from April to October 1971. I did not join the liberation combat forces. Instead, I organized a voluntary group to provide food and shelter as they (thousands, mostly Hindus) moved from place to place in remote areas to escape surprise military attack, with the help of local Islamists. Our job was to provide at least one meal a day. Sometimes, it was necessary to rob Muslim League leaders' houses for staples such as rice and lentil at night. They were hoarding Hindu property with the help of the military during the day. It was not an act of revenge. It was an act of humanity. I thought it was necessary to save lives—the greatest service I could offer during the human tragedy.

One day, the military invaded the village in Barisal but first announced via megaphone that they had come to start a peace initiative among villagers. They were asking Hindus to gather up in one place. Naturally, a lot of people responded to the fake call without realizing the danger behind it. Minorities always wanted to have peace with Muslim majority neighbors. It was in the vested interest of the military government to stand as obstacle. I was one of people who were curious to go out to face the military, but I changed my mind the last minute.

Next, I saw the military shooting at people. I saw men, women, and children running and screaming and falling on the ground and into the creek. I was about ten feet away from death by military bullet. I ran far away and climbed a big tree to hide from the prying eyes of the military, who were looking for Hindus. Then I realized how stupid I was; being in the tree would make me an easier target than a sitting duck. Fear had overwhelmed me. There was no place to hide. In a scene that you can only see in a movie, I came down from the tree and jumped into a pond, submerging my entire body except my nose so I could breathe. I stayed in that state for four hours.

When I got out, I could see and hear our Muslim neighbors ransacking the place where many Hindus had taken shelter. The group I'd befriended during the hideout in my aunt's house was nowhere to be seen. I wondered if I would ever see them alive again. I'd never imagined I could continue the fugitive life for a single day, but six months went by in the jungles of Barisal. Fears—that death could occur at any moment and for the welfare and whereabouts of my parents and siblings—occupied my mind. In fact, it was the thought of my family that kept me going. I thought someone would do Robin Hood work for my family in Sandwip, as I was doing similar work in the Barisal jungle.

During the revolutionary combats, I had the opportunity to cross the Indian border from Kaptai but decided to go home (to Sandwip) instead. But it was too risky to use any public transportation. The events had left me homeless, penniless, and riddled with frustrations and hopelessness. I ended up at my aunt's house in Barisal. For six months, I had stayed in those jungles, far from my island destination, Sandwip, facing imminent death at any moment. I'd thought about my parents and siblings every moment of that wild run.

Finally, after six months of living in a hellish environment, I decided to cross the border along with the elderly, children, and young girls. At that time, the Naxal movement, an internal terrorism by extreme communists, was at its peak in West Bengal. A distant relative who was a professor at the city college, H. L. Chatterjee, gave me shelter. In exchange, I volunteered to tutor his two young daughters. I also joined the Bangladesh government in exile in India. Slowly, the Naxal movement subsided during the Bangladesh movement—a positive outcome for the West Bengal government. The Naxal movement was scary at times. It was as if we had jumped from the frying pan to the fire.

Siddhartha Shankar Ray, central minister for Education and Youth Services (1971-1972), was a crisis manager for West Bengal under the leadership of the Prime Minister, Indira Gandhi. During the Naxal movement, West Bengal police had the standing order from the central government to shoot Naxal activists at night. But tactics they used were scary and many innocent young Bengalis fell victims. Naxal reference is important during that period. There was a regular curfew imposed at night warning young people not to go out. I did not have any choice. I used to walk from central Kolkata to North Kolkata at night after finishing my work at Mujibnagar. I did not have enough money to take public transportation. S. S Ray later served as the ambassador to the USA (1992-1996). Mr. Ray played a key role to improve the India-USA relationship during the critical period of his tenure. I did not know of any incident of refugee or freedom fighter casualty during the Naxal crisis in Kolkata. In fact, Naxal movement slowly died down when the Bangladesh revolution started.

Because I had no information from my parents, my personal life was chaotic and scary for the three months I spent in India, until Bangladesh was liberated. Things did not settle so easily even after liberation because random remnants of radical Islamism were present. It took more than a week to travel to my island from India because the prewar transportation system was not fully restored.

After the liberation of Bangladesh in December 1971, I visited my parents back home in Sandwip in January 1972 before going back to my workplace at Kaptai. My stay in Kaptai was also for a short period. From Kaptai, I left for Dhaka for the final preparation to go to Canada. It was an emotional moment. During the nine months of struggle, my parents had not known if I was alive or dead, just as I had not known of their situation. Seeing my parents was the most enjoyable moment of my life. It was not an easy task to see my sister, who had converted to Islam against the will of my parents.

My Muslim sister wanted to see me. I had to avoid that odd scenario though. She had written me many letters after she had settled in her life, but I did not respond to any of them. My friends taunted me, saying that my parents were saved by the influence of my sister and her Muslim husband.

In addition, I had to avoid the pressure from my parents to get married before going to Canada. Again, I wanted to establish myself—to build the stable life of my dreams before bringing someone into my life. It all worked well in the end. The only exception was the family had to be uprooted from Bangladesh, and we could not be all together at the same time in our ancestral home for traditional holidays and festive seasons.

Part II

Chapter 4

The Turtleback

I was born on a lush Island called Sandwip in the Bay of Bengal before the partition of India in 1947. The Island has the similar latitude as of Hawaii. Seen from above, Sandwip looks like the shell of a large turtle with algae growing from its back. Just like the rest of Bangladesh, the island is influenced by monsoon circulations and subject to cyclones and tidal waves. As a child, I would see three rounds of harvests and not just four but six distinctive seasons in a year. When the shifting pressure in the air fell upon our island, the beaches were submerged, crops damaged, and cattle killed. But farmers would rebuild from scratch every year, starting life anew as though natural calamity were only a part of the changing seasons.

I remember how pleasurable walking the entire length of the island was, passing banana, papaya, jackfruit, pineapple, and mango trees and eating from the sweet flesh of the island's abundance. The only difficulty was to board a ship to the mainland at Chittagong because there were no dockyards around the island. You had to get into a small rowboat to catch the ship. The risk of missing the boarding time and even getting washed out to sea was often unavoidable. At times, the elderly and the very young would die attempting to embark on the ship.

In 1961, when I was seventeen, a powerful cyclone hit Sandwip. Crops were damaged by saline water. At first, houses were destroyed, many people were killed, and cattle were washed away. Then a ship carrying over five hundred people from Chittagong to the island capsized, drowning its passengers. Soon, the cataclysm hit too close to home. The roof of our house collapsed, crushing my father and me inside it. I could hardly breathe. I didn't know if my father was alive until I heard him calling my name, and then I vomited blood from the injuries that had resulted when hundreds of pounds of metal sheets and wooden beams had knocked me down. Our neighbors arrived to rescue us, and my father and I escaped certain death.

Soon, my father, who was a doctor by profession, got up to treat the injured. In the aftermath of the rescue, we depended on USAID, along with aid from other organizations, for food. Strangely, it was not just famine we feared but the food that came from the sea—the island's most life-supporting resource. We could not eat fish for months because human fingers were discovered in the stomachs of several fish.

Calamities of the sea aside, my childhood was enjoyable—enjoyable until man-made catastrophes made the natural disasters child's play. Growing up, I was unaware of potential religious or political tension that was brewing across my homeland. I could never have imagined that my own friends from another faith would become the cause of my family's displacement. Situated in the same latitude as Hawaii, the island had the potential to be a resort for mainland and foreign travelers.

My father was a doctor, and my mother, a housewife. They gave me and my nine siblings, including my handicapped brother and sister, love and care. We played with the other kids, regardless of what their religious and ethnic backgrounds were. What united us was school and homework, which my peers often asked me to help with. We respected our teachers and, just like the other students, we didn't care who they were and what religion they belonged to.

Unfortunately, there were few educational opportunities for girls beyond elementary school. Even in elementary school, there were many restrictions placed on girls. They were not allowed to stay in class by themselves. They would be escorted in and out of class by a teacher. They would sit in the front two rows, and a select few boys—who were chosen by the teachers for demonstrating good behavior—would sit in the row behind them. I was one of those "good" boys.

Most teachers and parents followed the philosophy without knowing the great Nelson Mandela's name or his quotes on education and religion.

> Mandela's first quote, 'Education is the most powerful weapon you can use to change the world.'
> Mandela's second quote, 'our world is not divided by race, color, or religion. our world is divided into wise people and fools. And fools divide themselves by race, color, gender, or religion.'

But the thought of discrimination against children was alien to us. Then things changed overnight for us all after the military took over the country. Deadly race riots erupted as the military escalation between India and my country, still known as Pakistan, made us forget about the natural disasters. Sandwip was a pristine island situated in the same latitude as Hawaii. My first visit to Hawaii in late 1980 reminded me of the smell and the natural beauty of my birthplace—a potential tourists' heaven.

Chapter 5

Aiming For College

After graduating from high school in 1961 with excellent marks, I aimed at Comilla Victoria College, a college with a diverse heritage of culture. My brother, Bimal Kanti Chatterjee was completing his BA at Comilla. The city of Comilla was once a central place for Hindu culture with an interesting history. The famous Bengali poet Nazrul Islam married a girl from Comilla. The city was famous for sweets, ghee, and fresh butter. The sweets market attracted crowd of students and customers from all over the country. I also loved the history of Comilla. Many minority Hindu parliament members tried to take the government in the right direction, toward diversity and democracy. Among them, Dhirendra Nath Datta and Kamini Kumar Dutta, not related, stood out for their activism for democratic institutions in Pakistan.

For me, the best part of Comilla was the Iswar Pathsala residential high school for boys and girls. The place was established by scholar and philanthropist Mahesh Bhattacharya. Looking at the city, I always wished my sisters had been born there so they could receive a proper education. The first year of my college, I lived in a rental with other students in proximity to all these activities. The neighborhood of Kamini Datta's house had a big pond, and I used to take a bath there every morning before class. Kamini Datta's house was converted to a student residence.

As I was growing up, life felt normal to me under the protection and guidance of my parents. I had decided to follow in their footsteps from an early age. I was studying hard, with the simple goal of going to the mainland to ride in cars and trains. Riding airplanes was awfully expensive; but seeing planes fly was free of charge and would have been plenty—the naive dreams of a young boy in Sandwip!

What I did not know was that the British partition of India and Pakistan in 1947 would bring much more than the timber of my house crashing down upon me. It would bring the collapse of my very world. Frequent visits to the island from my college during holidays was agonizing when I discovered my friends were missing from the neighborhood and that I would not see them ever again. The phenomenon was more common during the early stage of the military ruling, when many discriminatory policies were enacted. Among these were a policy holding that no minority could be the head of state and the Enemy (Hindu) Property Act. By the power of the ACT the government would confiscate minority properties if any of the family member lived in India.

Dhirendra Nath Datta served as the minister of health and social welfare in East Pakistan (what is now known as Bangladesh). During the liberation war of 1971, he would be picked up by the military, along with his son, and the two of them would never be heard from again. They were probably tortured to death, as was the fate of many Hindu leaders in Pakistan. Kamini Kumar Dutta served as justice minister in the formative stage of Pakistan's constitution but died before Pakistan's instability as a nation began in earnest.

Chapter 6

Underwater Concealment

On a warm day in April 1971, a few days after I left my job at the age of twenty-seven, one village in Barisal Province was invaded by the military forces of our country, which was still known as East Pakistan. It was an act of violence the scale of which none of us had even heard of. I was at my aunt's house, together with near and far relatives, listening to the radio and gossiping, when we heard a bang outside. Through the window, I saw people screaming and running in every direction. They were pursued by soldiers in uniform. Upon seeing the military, I knew what was happening; they were there to kill Hindus. I could not just sit there and watch the slaughter of innocent people, so I considered confronting the soldiers face-to-face, even though I knew the massacre could not be stopped by words. When I stepped outside, I heard people shouting, "Army, army, killing, killing! Run away, run away!" I saw men, women, and children falling to the ground and into the creeks. The wake-up call hit me hard. How could I even think about talking sense into the murderous soldiers? I too ran as far as I could and then climbed a big tree to hide from the prying eyes of the soldiers who were looking for Hindus. Fear had overwhelmed me. There was no place to hide. I was confused and shivering with terror.

Then I realized my continued stupidity. Being up in a tree would make me an even easier target. I jumped down from the tree and hid behind a bush. An hour passed. I watched people flee, some carrying their belongings. I was terrified. But for some reason, I wanted to witness this atrocity. Next, to my horror, I saw local Islamists wearing the traditional loose outfits run toward my aunt's house. My maternal aunt was a daring and progressive woman. A widow, she was living with a boyfriend to protect the property she had inherited from her husband. Her only daughter was married to a professor in India. My aunt was sending all her earnings from the property to her daughter. She had a comfortable life both in Bangladesh and in India. When I met my aunt for the first time in 1968, she was suspicious of me. I met her on an official visit from my office. The objective was to meet all the villagers and record their grievances for compensation while directing a route for the construction of a high-voltage power line. She thought I might demand some share of her earnings because my mother came from the same family and, therefore, might have had some claim to the inheritance. Gradually, she knew I didn't have any personal interests, and she became very friendly. I used to see her often during my official tenure, from 1968 to 1970, and she would entertain me and my colleagues often with good food and words.

Now, fearing for my aunt, I noticed soldiers approaching. I jumped into the nearby creek. To breathe, I kept my nose above the water. My body was shivering beneath. The water was dirty; smelly; and, I knew, full of snakes. I remained quiet and motionless in the water. I would peek out from the water every now and then. I saw that the looters, encouraged by the killing carried out by the military, were taking everything from my aunt's house, including the window frames.

Once I'd ascertained that the immediate threat was gone, the looters now in the distance, I climbed out of the creek. With my drenched *lungi* dress wrapped around my waist, I ran amid a crowd fleeing to safety. It was growing dark. I was soaking, and there were no clothes to change into. I was afraid to enter my aunt's house. I saw other people running around holding their meager belongings over their heads. I followed them to the next shelter in a more remote place. I was safe but shocked.

I constantly thought of death. Nobody in my family would even know where I was. And that thought made me the saddest. I would find later that many other Hindu kids felt the same way. They were angry, desperate, and ready to do anything destructive to the brutal army and its supporters. I too was angry, but I thought of channeling my anger into a constructive force. That's when I learned about the freedom fighters. Those freedom fighters could be identified by their looks of fatigue. They were often in hiding. They would come to Hindu families in distress and talk to them in secret to assure their safety and security. They warned that the children must not scream during army operations, especially not in broad daylight. All able-bodied men were deployed to work in the fields to continue the production of food. In exchange, farmers would donate food to those displaced by the violence. Our strategy worked, and there was no disturbance in the camp except managing small children, for their screams would call forth terror.

Finally, a Hindu farmer took us in. Exhausted, I slept on the muddy floor with nothing to cover me. I wondered if I would ever see my parents again. Rumors spread among fleeing minorities that the military had first announced via megaphone that they had come for peace, asking Hindus to gather. Naturally, a lot of people had responded to the call; it was good for minorities to maintain peace with the Muslim majority military government. I had been one of those people curious to go hear what they had to say, but I had changed my mind at the last minute. Had I not changed my mind the rest would have been history—it would have been the end of my life.

━━━

The Pakistani military began their first round of killing as part of Operation Searchlight on March 25, 1971. Their primary targets were the leaders of the Awami League party, intellectuals, and minority Hindus. In the early stages of the operation, they amassed their victims in big cities with military cantonments (military headquarters in large cities, inside which initial killings were carried out once people had been arrested and transferred there) and naval bases such as Dhaka, Chittagong, and Khulna. Many of the Bengali regiments within the army or the police force were not trusted by those in the West Pakistani military. Indeed, some Bengali regiments revolted against the West Pakistani forces. There was another purpose for the cantonments—to interrogate and kill high-profile Hindu leaders and freedom fighters "caught in the act." The military would also torture these people to extract information against the army and about the hideouts of freedom fighters and disguised Indian soldiers. Catching Indian soldiers was like trophy hunting for Pakistanis—their successes a showpiece on the world's political stage. Many innocent people were victims of the process, which was never reported.

After such turmoil, West Pakistani forces attempted to bring stability to the big cities. Minorities, day laborers, civil servants, intellectuals, professors, and government workers—except Islamists and Pakistani supporters—fled the urban centers. But the army wanted to prove to the world that the country was under their control and that normalcy had resumed. In truth, the government hardly functioned; there was only the military's monopoly of violence everywhere one looked. After bringing the big cities under their tight control, the West Pakistani forces extended their brutal operations with help from many Islamist groups, especially at the border. "Peace" was the slogan the army used to lure their targets for killing. The military government controlled the media (radio and newspaper), and stories of such atrocities never got out. Even the foreign reporters were banned from visiting East Pakistan.

There was one bronze award-winning American army reporter on Vietnam, Mr. Joe Galloway, who visited Dhaka secretly and disguised himself, walking around critical areas to collect data. He even walked from a hotel to the US embassy to meet the then ambassador, Archer Kent Blood. Mr. Galloway (1941–2021) made an appeal to the ambassador against US policies in hopes of stopping the bloodshed in Bangladesh. His life story about Bangladesh was revealed by his wife, Dr. Gracie Galloway, at his memorial services held in Concord, North Carolina, September 2021.

The flow of refugees out of the country was another headache for the Pakistani military because India used it as a propaganda tool to garner support from the rest of the world. The United States, during the Nixon-Kissinger administration, refused to take any action against Pakistan. Instead, it supplied the Pakistani military with arms and ammunitions. The Nixon-Kissinger administration wanted to establish a link with China with Pakistan's help to diffuse the Russia-China axis. This and the refugee crisis caused many to take up arms. Militias were formed everywhere. The freedom fighters barely survived until support arrived from the Indian Army.

In early May 1971, the Pakistani army launched Operation Barisal, during which my friends and I hid. Using Barisal as its base, the army raided the surrounding villages with the help of local civilian Islamists. The Islamists were offshoots of various Muslim League Parties who opposed the liberation of Bangladesh. There were three distinctive names for them—Al-Badr, Razakar, and Al-Sham. All worked under the guidance of the military commander, General Amir Abdullah Khan Niazi, chief of the East Pakistan Army command. Among those three factions, Al Badr (mostly Bihari refugees from India during partition) was the most brutal toward Hindus. They spoke Urdu and had direct links with the army. Al Badr recruited members from local madrassas and accompanied the army on special operations in villages. Razakar and Al-Sham were Bengali Muslims who opposed liberation for the sake of Islam. But the army trusted Al Badr more than the other Islamists, and the majority of them left Bangladesh for West Pakistan on their own or via repatriation.

Three years later, it was painful to watch from abroad the slow demise of democratic freedom, especially for minorities. It was not due to autocrat West Pakistan anymore. It was due to our own Bengali military's despotism. I couldn't believe those forces indicated above, except that Al-Badr would be back to harass minorities again. I wasn't in the frontline action anymore to make critical decision, but the daily happenings during the crisis were always in the back of my mind, though I was busy building my career abroad. I remember the agony; the idea of quitting crossed my mind many times. But looking at the history and examples of great men who sacrificed their lives for a greater cause kept me going and kept others who followed me going. Here are two quotes that inspired me going forward with the mission:

1. Mahatma Gandhi, "The essence of civilization is to treat the uncivilized among us in a civilized manner."

2. Dale Carnegie, "Don't condemn, criticize or complain."

Yes, there was always doubt in my mind as to whether the high spirit and the positive attitude about the possibility of change and liberation we saw in people during the struggle could be maintained. Little did we know such phenomena would change overnight—when the founding father was assassinated. Civil war, or the liberation war, was the ultimate tool we had to use after we had tried peaceful protest and democratic election for the peaceful transfer of power. The commonsense approach did not work with the army.

In the beginning, I thought the human suffering would be over soon. That "soon" never came. I started counting hours and days. As each day passed, I was falling into a trap of confusion and uncertainty. The liberation meant a free country that had just been born. Everyone was trying to establish his or her importance in the country. That included both freedom fighter as well as pardoned Pakistani supporters. There was violent disruption to settle the difference and score points. The result was the assassination of the leader. We all were following the dream of the leader—a secular and progressive democracy away from Islamic domination. With the leader gone, the nation's dream died prematurely. Islamic domination became stronger by the day. Minorities started feeling disappointed and began leaving the country again because they were once again facing the same environment minorities had faced during the Pakistani regime. A strange and sad phenomena of human psychology that too many focused on grabbing power, instead of building the country with a common goal. There could've been several reasons behind such chaos.

Unfortunately, after the defeat of the army, all those Bangladeshis who committed atrocities along with the Pakistani army were arrested and promptly pardoned by the "benevolent" leader, Sheikh Mujibur Rahman, the founding father of Bangladesh. Those pardoned went on to commit a second round of atrocities against minorities; their wrath extended to the assassination of the sheikh himself. They would also Islamize the original secular and progressive constitution. They would keep the country in utter social and political ruin for a very long time—until the female leader, Sheikh Hasina, was democratically elected prime minister of Bangladesh in 2009. The Pakistani army and their civilian associates butchered innocent people indiscriminately in Bangladesh for over nine months, and the world watched, except India. The culprit military officers would not regret their atrocities, not even on their deathbeds. They would instead call for revenge against India, who defeated them and stopped the Hindu genocide. This period was a critical one in Bangladeshi history; after the death of the founding father, Islamization rose to the same level as it had been in Pakistan before the liberation. Hindus started migrating to India in large numbers again.

Chapter 7

My Stronghold

Barisal was a district in East Pakistan and is now a province in mainland Bangladesh across from Sandwip. It's the birthplace of the "Tiger of Bengal," or Shere-Bangla, A. K. Fazlul Huq, once the chief minister of an undivided Bengal under British rule. He was a lawyer by profession and a good parliamentarian. He entered politics during British rule and was active during the Bangladesh movement in support of Mujibur Rahman. He was well known as an orator of political speech, and that's how he survived as the longest-serving chief minister of an undivided Bengal. My mother is also from Barisal. She was born in the village neighboring Mr. Huq's.

When the killings started, I decided to go to Barisal, as I had acquaintances among the village leaders there due to my previous work. I was confident I could exploit those connections and resources to make useful contributions to our cause. After two weeks of traveling, I arrived in Barisal to find the city deserted. It was a ghost town. Rumor had it the military could return any day via the river port or by helicopter and kill anyone who'd stayed behind.

I began scouting around in Barisal. I wanted to find a secure place in remote areas to launch my personal mission against the past and forthcoming atrocities. I went to my aunt's house in Alta, close to Chakhar, the birthplace of A. K. Fazlul Huq. I had become friendly with Fazlul Huq's nephew, Mr. E. Karim, during the construction of a power line in the area. I knew he was a Muslim League (ML) supporter but thought he, being an elite of the area, may have changed his mind after the events that had shocked our nation and the world.

My aunt, Mrs. Roy Choudhury, was happy to see me. She now had a companion to protect her vast land inherited from the earlier feudal system, the Zamindari. She also sheltered many Hindu elite families with their teenage children. These families were lawyers, doctors, professors, and political leaders. There were fifteen to twenty people living there already. My aunt had hosted all of them with three meals a day for at least twenty days. I used my own cooking skills, learned as a high school student, when my father and I had lived together. We had a cook, but in the cook's absence, we had to cook for ourselves because Brahmins were not supposed to take food cooked by other casts.

Then on June 8, 1971, came the bombshell announcement of banning all five hundred and one thousand notes. Rich Hindus who had hidden their lifetime savings were hit the worst by the ban. It was easy to hide large amounts of cash in small bags with high-currency notes. There was no proper banking system. There was no trust in the financial institutions. The Hindus saved these large currencies for major life events, such as wedding ceremonies for their daughters. These rich Hindus were all individually at a loss, as they could not survive a day in hiding without such cash. They were also afraid to venture out to trade their notes in banks in the city. They were afraid of Islamists who might capture them on the way, find their hiding places, or kill them for their cash.

The military banned the notes to punish the minority Hindus because they knew many Hindus who carried such notes financially supported the freedom fighters. Finding no other way to save their money, many of these families trusted me with their cash and jewelry. I made a list of who I owed what. I hid jewelries around the house, memorizing the location of each one. The structure of my aunt's old house was an interesting one. There were many beams (ironwood) across the ceiling, ending in the brick walls. I thought these would make good hiding places for the jewelry, so I made little holes in those beams and there concealed these treasures. Some were on the ground around the house. All the wealthy people sheltering in my aunt's place had too much cash with larger bills. The cash or jewelry was their life savings, to be used for social events, such as a daughter's wedding. After the ban, they could not use their high value notes anymore. All those notes needed to be in the bank before the expiry date. I took the task on myself to save their cash—the source of prestige, pride, and social standing in the community.

A secret plan was prepared by all owners in consultation with me to rescue the cash. Three things had to happen to execute the plan – 1) A correct list of all owners with correct amount, 2) Transportation of the money to the Muslim friend. 2) Finding trusted Muslim partner or good Muslim Samaritan to take the money and deposit the money to the bank in their accounts.

The correct list was necessary to return the money to the rightful owner after the cash is saved and normalcy is returned. For transportation of money, I could not trust anybody else other than myself. I faked myself as a Muslim though I was not a Muslim. It took hours and days to practice Islamic rituals in Arabic for the road in case I face radical Muslims. One advantage I had was that I grew mustache and beard looking like a Muslim. I asked Muslim liberation fighters to teach me all rituals before, during and after the Islamic prayer. The worst disadvantage was I was not circumcised. I had to take a chance and overact on rituals. I also carried a bible to fake a Christian if needed depending on the situation. For trusting Muslim partners two names came to my mind. One was Enayet Karim, principal of Fazlul Huq College (1960-1978), founded by his uncle Shere-Bangla Fazlul Huq. Mr. Karim, I thought, was indebted to me for granting many of his requests for the electrification of the college and the surrounding villages. There was a competing AL leader in charge of a school in Mr. Karim's neighboring college. (I forgot his name; I call him Mr. X). I knew I had to walk several miles to see Mr. Karim, a risky venture irrespective of the day or time of the day. Despite rigorous preparation, I never knew the role nervousness would play in a real situation. Luckily, I never had to face that challenge. I had to borrow a lungi, one kurta, and one Muslim cap.

Mr. Karim had a selfish reason for developing friendship. He became a trusted friend during the days I oversaw establishing a power distribution center at the college. On the other hand, I did not have a chance to develop a close relationship with Mr. X. Fortunately during the crisis, he turned out to be the best friend one can expect – 'a friend in need is a friend indeed.'

I didn't have any idea that we'd be uprooted forever and would never return to the place where we were hiding. At least for me, I never had that opportunity to meet and greet those people who helped me during the struggle after the liberation.

There was no other option available to us but to trust each other from that point onward. This was the first challenge or opportunity for me to make a difference. I had to prepare how I would reach the locals and displaced people—what and how I would tell them. I went in disguise as a Muslim, carrying the cash around in a large sack to find the right individual.

Mr. Enayet Karim was a Muslim League supporter. I was overconfident to get his support. Nervous, I met him in the bazaar, where he told his assistant to lead me to his bungalow (a house for an outside visitor). As soon as I had entered his house, he disappeared. Later that night, I heard a knock at the door. I hoped it was Mr. Karim. Surprisingly, the same peon came with a dinner plate and a sealed note from Mr. Karim. The note reads, 'Chatterjee Babu, I do not wish to see you here in the morning'.

I was caught off guard. The response was cruel and heartbreaking. I had thought Mr. Karim was a friend. I had been in his house many times before the conflict. But here he had left no room for discussion. Then I thought to myself that it could have been worse. He could have sent someone to hurt me or asked the police to arrest me, given that Hindu killing had become the norm.

I got up early in the morning and headed to the other AL leader I knew four or five miles away. I had to walk, so I chose early morning, before sunrise. My legs shook, as I carried heavy bags full of five hundred- and one thousand-rupee banned banknotes in this period of lawlessness. I went alone so as not to put anyone else's life at risk.

I went directly to the AL leader's home, where he was performing his morning prayers and having breakfast. The AL leader was sitting in a chair in his drawing room. He stood up, grabbed my hand, and hugged me as soon as he saw me and started crying. Tears were rolling down his cheek. "Chatterjee Babu?" he said. "You can stay with us, and nobody will hurt you as long as we are alive."

I gave him the list of persons the money belonged to. He called his son to be a witness. He also asked his son to be responsible for depositing the money in their accounts and keeping the list of who the money belonged to. He then called a boat and headed to the bank in town. Hopefully, the gentleman knew the guideline designed by the military to deposit such high currency notes—no Hindu name, of course. I was not on the list because I did not have any money. Years later, after I had settled in Canada, I found out that every single person who'd entrusted their fortunes to me had gotten every rupee returned to them.

When the day was over, I went back to my aunt's home and called everybody to tell them of my venture for the day. They were surprised to see me home safe. It was a moral boost for all, of course. We were, again, somehow leading a normal routine—listening to the BBC and Akashvani (Kolkata) after a day's work of looking out for the army and Islamists. It was interesting to identify both groups—one by their army fatigues and the other by an Islamic cap and a lungi (a traditional Islamic dress for men in Bengal). The final news said Barisal was on West Pakistan's radar from the beginning because of its importance as a river port for transporting arms and ammunition. But the freedom fighters, the Mukti Bahini, kept it under their control.

Several days later, more people joined us far out from the army's reach. We formed a group of young volunteers to take care of each other and fight for the liberation of Bangladesh—with arms or with no arms. All of us were not a combat force but a troop of cheerleaders to keep moral of thousands of people high, to provide security and safety in the camp, and to feed those in the camp. We also served as a kind of vanguard within our camps. Girls and women were vulnerable not just to the army but to other within the camp itself. Even though everybody maintained honesty, civility, and dignity within the camp voluntarily. We kept an eye out for all. It was almost like believing in the English folklores of Robin Hood and his Merry Men. I was one of the most educated young individuals in the camp of several hundreds. There was no robbery and no theft. We prepared ourselves to pretend to be Christians or Muslims when necessary. It was astounding to observe how sincerely people could respond when facing death collectively.

Unfortunately, all gems and jewelries were lost after the military raid. Nobody could return to the house, as militants and radicals took full control of the house after the military crackdown in that Barisal village. That did not deter us from regrouping and pursuing our mission in further remote areas.

That is how the four pillars of Bangladesh's initial democracy were developed in the initial constitution—nationalism, socialism, democracy, and secularism. Unfortunately, Bangladesh could never live up to its democratic standards because of the influence of Islamization, which exists even today.

Chapter 8

A Page From Robin Hood

I read the story of Robin Hood in my childhood. Over the course of years, I became a believer of the proverb, "Man proposes and God disposes." My father used to tell me how to earn respect from people you wished to serve. He advised me to develop trust and confidence by example. That's what he did throughout his whole life, though neither the society nor the country treated him well at the end of his life—a sad ending. My father had a unique position serving the islanders as a doctor. Many residents, irrespective of religion, respected him like a saint. Of course, there were some oddball Muslim fanatics, especially women and girls at the instigation of those fanatics, who were reluctant to see him because, in their minds, seeing a Hindu doctor was against Islam. Those types of people caused worries for my mother, with her young girls, the most.

As the months went by, I realized we were here for the long haul. My Muslim friend from the Awami League Party introduced me to the local communities. They were smart enough not to introduce me as an engineer. Knowing the Christian community was immune from large-scale brutality, I arranged for a cross to hang around my neck, and I carried a Bible in a sack wherever I went. I started working with peasants in the paddy fields and vegetable gardens. You could say I became a day laborer. I had to forget my engineering profession. But internally, I used my engineering knowledge of process improvement for harvesting and planting new crops—distributing work, stacking output, carrying to a mechanized house, and stacking the final product for storage. I worked hard and honestly. The family who employed me found a day's work completed in a shorter time. People listened to me. I took this opportunity to develop a command over them.

I wanted to form a group of trusted individuals to do the dirty work for me. It could have sounded dirty in normal days, but to me and to many others, it was a necessity for that moment to preserve the dignity and civility of human life. It wasn't easy to disclose my intention. I spent many agonizing days and didn't have proper sleep for nights in a row. I looked at the families and their children in distress and gathered some courage to stand up and decide what to do. I couldn't do it openly. I selected a small number of individuals I could trust. I confided in them my plan and asked for their help. I couldn't believe their enthusiasm and excitement. I articulated a simple message to denounce the army's action in the language of the village. I told them clearly that saving lives irrespective of ethnicities was God's will, and we should all work for it, though I didn't believe in any god myself.

One day, I whispered to someone that they could fight with us to save minority lives from the Pakistani army and to liberate Bangladesh. The response was overwhelming. Word spread to neighboring villages. I insisted that everyone keep the plan secret. I assigned tasks. I delegated missions. I was becoming an undercover leader. The news spread, and freedom fighters volunteered their help with arms and ammunitions. I did not want my volunteers to be armed but kept the option of accepting the freedom fighters' help when needed. I did not want any infighting among us, given the environment was one of complete lawlessness. It looked as if intellectual might was right. It was hard to believe what I was seeing.

Soon, other freedom fighters in the area offered us rifles, but we decided not to carry them. We couldn't trust them. It might've been a setup. We had volunteers among us who were trained to collect food items to feed refugees hiding from the army. In fact, after a few days, they were ready to do anything within their means to fight for our cause. They surveyed the area first to understand who was doing what and how. They collected data by talking to various sources. Local bazaars were the main source. There, we could identify stolen materials and who had stolen them. Sometimes, rich individuals employed poor villagers to sell materials on their behalf. After several days, our men knew the movement of Muslim males supporting the Pakistani army. Our volunteers began to attack their houses, often at night, when the males were gone. We ran drills. After a few successful trials, we expanded our operations across different villages, stealing from the rich and feeding thousands of children, adults, and elderly and providing them cover as they ran from house to house. All of us were on a constant move for our safety and security. We carried the sick and relocated the injured to safer, more remote places. Volunteers became innovative. Four people with two bamboo sticks and a sack made of old clothes hanging in between them could carry an individual wherever he or she intended to go, sometimes great distances. For short distances, the elderly were carried on the backs of volunteers. The technique was especially helpful for crossing borders with disabled individuals. Of course, some of them could not survive the exhaustion, lack of food and constant move.

The volunteer groups we formed had many functions—chief among them preparing food and feeding the homeless at least one meal a day in the morning or at night so that all could be free for the rest of the day to assist those in need with evading the troops and the Islamists. Children were fed first and then the adults. I was amazed how little people asked for. For example, in a family of four with two adults and two children, parents would be happy with one piece of bread and would ask for two pieces for the children. Some parents would sacrifice their shares for the children of others. We didn't ration the food if we had enough for at least one full meal for each.

I lost twenty-five pounds in six months, due to the food shortage and running around, looting the houses of those Islamists who had sided with the army. We stole rice and lentils. It was never our intention to kill the Islamists, though a few chosen leaders carried revolvers given to us by the freedom fighters. Each family might venture out for raw vegetables and fruits and would share their harvest with the rest as much as possible. Cooperative mantras were instilled in everybody, and it was an effort on everyone's part to maintain it.

We had arms available to us to fight the army, but unfortunately, those arms were no match against the tanks and machine guns of the army. Instead of combating the army on a level we could not win, I negotiated with the freedom fighters to take care of the elderly, women, and children. Managing internal chaos and feeding so many was a challenge. Combative Bangladeshi liberation forces didn't interfere with my operation; rather, they cooperated as much as they could for its success. My role in the liberation struggle was like running a government administration.

Potable water saved lives. Luckily, tube wells were available a short walk from the camp. Earthen pots were used to store the water that was rationed for those who couldn't walk easily to the well. Children were helpful in pumping water from the well and filling bigger pots for everyday use, such as cooking and washing. We used banana leaves as plates to serve food. We used dead plants as fuel for cooking fires. We fed hundreds at a time, a combination of rice, lentils, and locally sourced vegetables. Getting rid of human waste was a challenge. Men went to the creeks, canals, or rivers. Women were watched by other women.

People became self-disciplined and trustworthy. At times, emotions and anxieties flared. Doctors, lawyers, and others in the group would jump in to take care of adverse situations. Luckily, nothing went out of control during the six months I oversaw the operation. It was hoping against hope that we could ever bring back that civility, dignity, and self-respect that had existed during the army operation following the liberation of the country; there was the foundation of four pillars of the Bangladesh constitution—nationalism, socialism, democracy, and secularism. Unfortunately, all were over and forgotten in less than three years after the assassination of the founding father, Sheikh Mujibur Rahman.

Slowly, groups were thinning out in the camp. People were leaving the country, as life had grown unbearable. There was the slow disappearance of the Pakistani army and an increased resurgence of freedom fighters. In addition, the presence of the Indian Army gave us considerable hope. Indian soldiers dressed in plain clothes guarded the borderlands. They spoke in local languages so nobody would suspect them of being Indian agents before war was declared by Indira Gandhi, prime minister of India, on December 3, 1971. Fortunately, the war was over by December 16, 1971. It was with a sigh of relief that I heard Indira Gandhi's speech in person at the Kolkata racecourse. I wish I could have relayed the message of hope and assurance by Ms. Gandhi to the rest of the displaced people and those trapped in the jungle. I was sure they had heard it on the BBC or Akashvani Kolkata (Debdulal Bandopadhyay)—the only source of authentic news during the crisis.

Survival came at different costs for different people. One family, the Mukherjees, converted to Islam to escape the misery and headed to the city. The Mukherjees, with two parents and one teenage boy and one teenage girl, was a respectable business family from the city of Barisal. Mr. Mukherjee, who converted to Islam, was protected after their daughter agreed to marry a Muslim boy. It was a one-sided irony that the Mukherjee family's boy was not asked to marry a Muslim girl.

Chapter 9

Turning Turbans

During the War of Liberation, the Muslim population of Bangladesh was divided between two parties, ML (Muslim League) and AL (Awami League) mostly. The Hindu population, having no other choice, threw its support behind AL. But their preference was the National Awami Party (NAP), founded by Moulana Bhasani. NAP was progressive and had an unbiased social vision for the society.

In addition to Islam and Hinduism, there were two other religions predominant in Bangladesh—Christianity and Buddhism. Christians and Buddhists supported AL because they were against the military administration and its discriminatory laws based on religion. Buddhism was limited to a tribe in Southeast Bangladesh close to Myanmar. Christianity could be found throughout Bangladesh. Each of these religions played different political roles at different times. But Hindus could never be in the good book of Pakistani military leaders because of relations between India and Pakistan in the aftermath of partition. Rumors circulated that the Pakistani military was not killing Christians only to keep the United States on their side. There was no way to verify this rumor. It did not matter, however, because surviving by any means was the mantra. Immediately, I saw an opening to enhance my chances of survival—knowing all rituals of both Islam and Christianity. Pretending to be Christian was not hard. You carried a cross and recited psalms from the Bible. In other words, it was as simple as pretending to love Christ and your neighbor as yourself. There was no way the Pakistani military could verify or authenticate your Christian identity. To be a Muslim, there were eleven ritual steps to prepare for the prayer, pray, and finish the prayer. There were Arabic verses you must perform in each step. The troubling part was the military could easily verify and authenticate every verse you uttered and its chronology.

There was some correlation between the Awami League (AL) party and the Muslim League party in principle and philosophy. AL was an offshoot of ML, founded in 1949 after the partition by original Muslim League leaders, such as Shahid Suhrawardy and Yar Mohammad Huq. East Pakistani Muslim League leaders wanted to differentiate themselves from West Pakistani Muslim League leaders for the jurisdictional identity of east and west. On the other hand, Sheikh Mujibur Rahman was a strong follower of Shahid Suhrawardy and spearheaded all party activities. He became the leader of the party after Suhrawardy's death.

Abdul Hamid Khan Bhashani was also a founding member of the Muslim League before he formed his own leftist party called National Awami Party (NAP), which differed from AL or ML both in principle and philosophy. East Pakistan Students Union (EPSU) aligned with NAP more than AL. EPSU was the epicenter of both progressive Muslim and minority students. AL leader Sheikh Mujibur Rahman demanded East Pakistan federation under the central Pakistan. In early years of the movement, he did not want to separate from Pakistan. The Agartala Conspiracy of 1966 against Sheikh Mujibur Rahman dampened his ideal of a united Pakistan, resulting in many unofficial changes in the party platform. Students' movements reinforced Mr. Rahman's radical thoughts on East Pakistan, which led to the liberation of Bangladesh.

In 1970 and onward, minorities (among students and the public) gave full support to AL. During the 1971 crackdown by the Pakistani army, all AL leaders fled to India and formed the Bangladesh government in exile. India was willing to support the Bangladesh movement when uncontrollable refugees began crowding its West Bengal border with East Pakistan. In exchange, India demanded a secular and progressive constitution with full protection of minority rights and the restoration of minority properties. This is reflected in the twelve-point 1972

India-Bangladesh Treaty of Friendship, Cooperation and Peace, signed by Indian prime minister Indira Gandhi and Bangladesh prime minister Sheikh Mujibur Rahman.

I knew even then that religion, mixed with politics and social issues, became a weapon capable of destroying humanity. Much later, after living in the West for fifty years, I would develop the conviction that religion is the root cause of millions—if not billions—of deaths in the world. If religious people take control of politics, it becomes a double-edged sword for the populace beneath them. Religious slogans like, "Religion is for mutual love and peace," become ridiculous when humanity is taken into consideration. Religious people in power ignite discrimination and polarization on social or political issues, creating a hatred environment.

India, under prime minister Indira Gandhi, began lobbying foreign leaders on behalf of Bangladesh. Many countries, such as the USSR (which was the second country to recognize Bangladesh after India), responded favorably. Bangladesh was indebted to Indira Gandhi's leadership from start to finish. India might have had a vested interest in the total collapse of Pakistan as a nation. But providing the proper leadership, especially against the United States of America, during this tumultuous time was singularly brave and praiseworthy. Bangladesh would not have been liberated in such a short period without Indira Gandhi's leadership.

During the aforementioned period, minorities were motivated to provide full support behind AL and wanted full liberation of Bangladesh. I was glued, together with others, to the Akashvani broadcasting center from Kolkata, perceiving that the news was authentic and interpreting that Bangladesh may be liberated—the last hope of minorities. It was my analysis and conviction from different evidence on the ground and official news spread by different radio stations. Our interpretations of news and events encouraged many others to keep going, though they did not have three meals a day or a normal life. Slowly, people were convinced that Pakistan could not win, but the fate of liberation and its timing was anybody's guess.

The Awami League Muslim leader who'd helped me to cash banned currency notes understood my empathy and requested that I pretend to be Christian in case of any danger. This person was also in danger because of his political and religious philosophy. It was interesting how I was rejected by one ML friend (presumed the better friend with political connections) but welcomed by another AL acquaintance (who was not that well known), who helped me to deposit all the banned currencies I brought him. He asked me to practice Christianity just in case. He was very honest. He could have asked me to practice Islam but thought Christianity would be simpler for two reasons. One was Pakistan's good relationship with the United States. And the other was that Christianity was simpler to practice with less understanding of its indelicacy by the army. On the other hand, for extra security from Islamists before the journey with all the cash in a sack, I'd practiced Islamic rituals with Arabic verses for prayer and hoped the army would not be active enough to ask for the recitation in the weary hour of the day. The other danger was if the army checked the circumcision.

Chapter 10

Thinking Right From Wrong

My decision to leave the job at Kaptai was to avoid the initial thrust from the army. I was sure I would need to abscond only for a short period, as had been the case in the past under similar protests and disruptions of government administration. In hindsight, I see that decision was perfect, as it was taken exclusively out of fear for my life. There was public unrest, as the military jailed, killed, tortured, and raped. Many newspapers and radio reports circulated the details of these brutal atrocities. My intention was to spend a few quiet days in a remote village of the island and return to work after it was all over. I felt after a month or two, things would return to normalcy as had happened previously. In fact, the military seized control of big cities before the Indian forces started providing support to different freedom fighters. That was an emotional setback I could never overcome as I was moving village to village. I could not imagine the army would be so crude and shrewd as to kill and torture its own citizens. They did it by organizing a national militia to do the army's dirty work all over East Pakistan, starting first in the big cities and then moving on to the remote areas.

I was wrong. The formation of a militia to control protests without the transfer of power based on the election result had never happened on previous occasions starting from the language movement of 1952. Looking at the grim view of killing and destruction, I decided to leave my job site. It was easier to roam around the country with many unknowns, rather than to face the death by army squads I had witnessed with my own eyes. One of the many unknowns was whether or not I would be able to unite with my parents and siblings or see them alive.

The other unknown was when normalcy would come and what it would look like, if it came at all—farming, education, industrial production? Farmers were afraid to participate in normal farming for crops. Students stopped going to schools and colleges. Industry stopped producing goods. Everything came to a standstill.

Despite that setback, I was convinced things would return to normal. I thought I would be back to the job within months. Little did I know, such roaming would lead me to a nightmare that would last for over six months. During the liberation, I was a young twenty-six-year-old man with big dreams. I had everything to succeed—family, education, job, and ambition. Initially, I thought all would be over in months, if not a few days. So, taking a shelter in remote village would be safer for a short time before things returned to normal. Yes, my initial thought reflected my view that the army would win the battle.

During those six months in the jungle, I tried to reflect on and understand human existence. I was inspired to love my country by a famous quote by Giuseppe Mazzini: "A country is not a mere territory; the particular territory is only its foundation. The country is the idea which rises upon that foundation; it is the sentiment of love, the sense of fellowship which binds together all the sons of that territory." I thought of it over and over for inspiration, not only for me but also for all who had confidence in me. It was emotionally exhausting and physically tiring. The conclusion I came to was that it was not a crime to revolt against illegal, inhuman, and arbitrary mass killing. The conflict had been imposed on us and a fair resolution by any means was the determination of my young mind.

Part III

Chapter 11

College and Engineering (1961–1967)

I was unknown to the class and the community I was living in nearby my college, which contrasted with the island living, where I used to know all my neighbors, teachers, and others by name, family, and occupation. I had free access to meet anybody. Sometimes, I missed that island environment in my new living. To compensate my loneliness or the gap of ever-present neighbors, I became creative. I organized a "night watch group" with students who were living close by in Comilla. The responsibilities of the group were to know all the neighbors, help those neighbors who were in need, and prevent petty theft. Petty theft included stealing fruits and vegetables from neighbor's yard or unlawful entry inside the house. It was basically supplementing police work. All members were required to spend one hour every night and visit the designated neighborhood and assure their presence. Our work was highly appreciated by all residents, especially older female residents in the community. Members of night watch group were occasionally rewarded with home-cooked food by ladies of the community. With such treatment, everybody felt at home far away from home. In the process, we got into some innocent mischief as well, for example, harmlessly teasing girls or stealing some ripe mangoes—a delight during the summer night.

Then came the first year-end national exam. My achievements were among the top three in the class. That standing drew the attention of many professors and students, mostly from the science and math courses—my favorite subjects. Among the professors who accepted me among elite students beyond their known circle were Khitendra Kumar Roy, Monindra Dev, and Rajjab Ali of the mathematics department and P. K. Roy, Khurshid Alam, and Jyotsnamay Dutta of the physics department. I was also well respected by other elite students.

In my second year of the college, I moved to the college residence to be part of a bigger group. Since that attention, I had full access to all professors' help as and when needed. In fact, I took lots of help from them. The result was I was one of the top ten in the Comilla board final exam. Professor P. K. Roy had one son, Arun K. Roy, who was our classmate. We spent many hours together in their residence in a family environment, with good food and other recreational treats. Arun Roy completed his doctorate of philosophy in the United Kingdom and settled there.

All my excitement about getting into the engineering college was becoming shadowy as event after event (social, religious, and political) was complicating the lives—even the existence—of minorities both on and off campus. It started with the quota system. The quota system prevented many minority students from being admitted though their scores were higher than many majority Muslim students who were admitted. It was all joy and pride as I started the first year of the engineering college. There was a total of thirty-nine minority students in the first year, which included some architectural students as well. There were a similar number of minority students in the other three senior years. Every one of those students was smart and intelligent. All of us were on a four-year, fully paid scholarship to pursue engineering degrees. It was always rewarding and entertaining to interact and exchange ideas with these students.

All Hindu students were residents of a joint Hindu-Muslim hostel but with a separate kitchen where no beef was served. We randomly chose our roommates, mostly Hindus, three in a room. In the class, relations between Hindus and Muslims were cordial as well initially. Things started going downhill during my second year, after the 1964 communal race riot and other events following the race riot. My first year had been, overall, uneventful, with a good academic result. My second year was the year to select a major. I chose electrical engineering. It was tough to go through the next three years of engineering (from

1964 to 1967). Fortunately, I met one professor in the department of electrical engineering, Arifur Rahman, who guided me through the next three years successfully. He also wrote all my recommendations letters for admission in international schools. I must credit him for my success. I owe him what I am now. Mr. Arifur Rahman settled in the United States of America after the Bangladesh liberation, which I came to know much later. I wanted to meet him personally, but that never materialized because of his premature death.

Chapter 12

The 1964 Race Riot

In January 1964, a communal riot started in Dhaka, Narayanganj, and other surrounding areas. It quickly spread in all other districts such as Chittagong, Khulna, Mymensingh, and so on in East Pakistan. Biharis (displaced Muslims from the state of Bihar, India) and other Urdu-speaking residents (Nawab descendants) started to indiscriminately persecute Hindus in response to an alleged theft of the prophet's hair from the Hazratbal Shrine in Jammu and Kashmir, India. This situation was further aggravated by President Ayub Khan's statement at Dhaka airport: "I won't be responsible for any reaction in Pakistan due to the Hazratbal incident." The statement was further supported by Abdul Hai, a member of the Advisory Committee of the Islamic Board. In addition, the Pakistan Convention League declared Kashmir Day on January 3, 1964, and the situation became worse for all minorities.

Unfortunately, it was reported later that the whole Hazratbal epic was doubted based on Pakistan's fake propaganda on the radio. The salient feature of the incident was the selective destruction of Hindu-owned industries and merchant establishments in many cities.[3] This resulted in ever-unending Hindu refugees in West Bengal. It was a national problem in India, and refugees were resettled in Dandakaranya of Odisha and Madhya Pradesh.

I, like many of other Hindu university students, crossed the border to explore education possibilities while becoming a refugee in West

---

[3] Wikipedia, s.v. "1964 East Pakistan Riots.", January, 1964. Bhattacharyya, S.K. (1987). *Genocide in East Pakistan/Bangladesh.* Houston: A. Ghosh. p. 89. ISBN 0-9611614-3-4.

Bengal. Prafulla Chandra Sen was then the chief minister of West Bengal. Triguna Sen was the vice chancellor of Jadavpur University. Both Sens worked together to work out a formula to admit all displaced students from East Pakistan but with no guarantee of financial support. Almost all of the refugee students were admitted to universities across West Bengal (engineering or other). Looking at the family's financial situation and given I would have no financial backing to continue my engineering education in India, I returned to Dhaka. It was a tough decision after watching the destruction of Hindu property and the massacre of human lives. Luckily, none of my close family relatives was hurt, but all our properties were damaged. Psychological and emotional damage still haunts the family members.

I vowed to pursue a PhD program in Canada or the United States at any cost after finishing my bachelor's degree in electrical engineering. Little did I know what other adverse calamities were in front of me. Only nine out of the thirty-nine first-year Hindu students returned. I guess nine made a decision to mine. Unfortunately, we found out one or two fellow students and kitchen staff had been killed while trying to escape from the dorm. We returned, but the situation at the dorm had changed. We were harassed harshly by fellow Muslim students, as well as some Muslim professors daily. We had to keep our emotions low, always maintaining our cool and ignoring all adverse encounters, focusing on a single mission—to graduate.

Hindu-Muslim tension was high and race riots were very frequent in Pakistan, more so in East Pakistan than West Pakistan. East Pakistan had a larger Hindu population than did West Pakistan. That was why Hindus in East Pakistan were always targeted by the military. Naturally, they reasoned, this would result in greater casualties of Hindus and more migration to India—which would ultimately lead to either the elimination of Hindus or their conversion out of fear.

Hindu-Muslim tension existed during the British rule. This was because Muslims (radicals) boycotted English education after losing power to the British, while Hindus embraced British rules and cooperated fully with them for political, social, and economic favor. Hindus had coexisted with Muslims under the Muslim administration many years before the British came to India. The British took over the Indian administration from Muslim rulers, and that was a sore point for Muslims, resulting in their demanding a separate country for themselves. Muslims stopped cooperating with the British rule. They could not tolerate an upper hand of the India Congress Party (ICP) dominated by Hindus.

The Muslims misused their opportunity after a separate country was granted to them. Instead of rebuilding a nation and looking after their people, they focused on war with India to be a bigger power. It was not necessary at all for the better good of the country and its people.

If we look back many years in the history, in most situations, the Pakistani army or police would delay actions against criminals, causing much death and destruction in the community. The 1964 riot was no exception. The real cause of the riot was an allegation that the hair of the Muslim prophet, Muhammad, was missing from the Hazratbal Shrine in Srinagar, Kashmir.[4] Further fuel was added when the Pakistan Muslim League declared January 3, 1964, as a Kashmir day. The consequence was indiscriminate killing of Hindus, looting and burning houses, forced conversion, and the abduction and rape of young girls. Casualties resulted from inactions on the part of the government. What does a Kashmir problem have anything to do with Hindu minorities in East Pakistan other than the persecution of innocent people?

To my direct knowledge, one classmate was going to see his parents in Narayanganj, a river city to Dhaka, to celebrate the Bengali thanksgiving holidays. He was picked up from the bus and killed right at the bus station.

My uncle was so disgusted with the situation that he fled his home with all his family members and went to India. They settled in the Dandakaranya region of Odisha and Madhya Pradesh. I found out they were gone when I visited home from college. I never saw them again in their lifetime. I am in touch with my uncle's surviving family members now, but he died several years back. They have their children

---

[4] US Central Intelligence to Consolidate Agency, 1964 Report; Nevard Jacques, "Riots Arouse Muslim Shame," *New York Times*, January 24, 1964.

and grandchildren, but I never saw any of them. The curse falls on humanity when a country cannot take care of its citizens simply for political reasons.

The brewing of civil war started with the 1952 language movement. Hindus had a truly small role in the initial movement. Jinnah wanted Urdu to be the state language, but East Pakistanis, led by Sheikh Mujibur Rahman, wanted Bengali to be recognized as another language. Minorities paid dearly for the strong position taken by the Awami League (AL) led by Sheikh Mujibur Rahman. The military wrongfully assumed AL was being influenced by Hindu intellectuals and India. We observed such a sensation during the disastrous communal riot of 1964 in East Pakistan.

In 1963 (our batch), thirty-nine minority students (part of a minority quota) were admitted to the Ahsanullah Engineering College, but only nine minority students returned after the holiday following the communal riot during the second year. In fact, more Hindu students could have been admitted if there was no quota. Traditionally, Hindus were more progressive and educated than majority Muslims because Muslims had boycotted cooperation with British rule. The nine students who returned were:

1. Teen Kori Barua (architect), Bangladesh
2. Niranjan Bhakta, bachelor of science, engineering (EE), Bangladesh, now deceased
3. Amalendu Chatterjee, PhD (computer communications), United States of America
4. Aparesh Das (architect), Bangladesh, now deceased
5. Uzzal Kanti Das, bachelor of science, engineering (EE), Bangladesh
6. Haran Karmaker, PhD (power), United States of America
7. Radhika Ranjan Roy, PhD (network and communications), United States of America
8. Bangshi Badan Saha, PhD (engineering), United Kingdom
9. Nani Gopal Saha, bachelor of science, engineering ((EE), Bangladesh, retired, lives in Canada with his children

All of us who were admitted in 1963 had the privilege of scholarships for four years of engineering education. It was similar for other year students as well. The 1964 communal disturbance caused many of us to go to India to explore an alternative way to continue our studies. For some, this was not financially feasible. The rest had financial means and took the privilege of the Indian government's help to continue their engineering or other education. It was not an easy return to the class by all of us who went to India, but we had to return to the class.

When we did so, we were humiliated by our classmates, as well as by some professors. The nine of returning classmates formed a strong bond like a family and became successful in our life struggles later. The Muslim students doubled down on us when the 1965 war started. And we, along with our Hindu seniors, were determined to finish our studies at any cost. I am in touch with many of them even today. Some of them died, and some settled in Western countries with their successful grown-up children.

Chapter 13

1965 War And Agartala Conspiracy

As we were settling for the second-year engineering the second blow of disruption came—this time in the form of the 1965 war between India and Pakistan. This was the second war India and Pakistan fought over Jammu and Kashmir. The first war (October 1947) established the line of control over Kashmir between two countries under UNSC arbitration. Pakistan's aim was to recapture India in order to establish an Islamic region like the Ottoman Empire. Negotiation, as compared to direct conflict, could have given Pakistan more socioeconomic and political leverage. I think this conflict started the power struggle among all Muslim League leaders, instead of building the nation. The result was Pakistan became a failed state—and remains so as of this writing today. In the 1965 war, General Ayub Khan developed a different strategy based on Kashmiris discontentment with Indian rule and on the loss by India in the 1962 Chinese war. After some success in the Rann of Kutch skirmish (on the West Pakistan border) by Pakistan, General Ayub Khan secretly launched "Operation Gibraltar.[5] Pakistan's strategy of sending infiltrating saboteurs to win the heart of Kashmiris was discovered, and Pakistan lost the war.

The impact of the war on East Pakistan was devastating for Hindu students, student movements, and AL leader Mujibur Rahman alike. Mujib's character was not portrayed as one of the progressive political leaders that existed in the East Pakistan. The Agartala Conspiracy and then the denial of handing over the power to the rightfully elected

---

[5] Wikipedia, s.v. "Operation Gibraltar"; Victoria Schafield, *Kashmir in Conflict: India, Pakistan and Unending War* (I. B. Tauris, 2003).

candidates like Mujib made him more of an activist for the liberation when the military crackdown against innocent people started.

We minority students were under the careful watch of our Muslim classmates, confined in one corner of our hostel (the Hindu residence). We were not allowed free movement. Going to the rooftop or carrying a flashlight were no-nos. One of our classmates was arrested for such a violation. He was reported to the army and was taken away from the residence. He was not seen again after the war. He was probably killed by the army. The poor student suffered from nyctophobia (fear of darkness) and that cost him his life. All of us endured humiliation after humiliation during the rest of our study years. We were counting down the days for our study to be over.

Then came the Agartala Conspiracy (also known as "Shorojantra Mamla" in Bengali) against AL leader Sheikh Mujibur Rahman. Agartala was a city in Tripura, India, northeast of Bangladesh. Thirty-five Bangladeshis, including Mujibur Rahman and many army personnel, were accused of meeting with the Indian Army to sabotage Ayub's regime. The conspiracy theory against Sheikh Mujibur Rahman as an Indian agent provided a relief of tension among minority students. The progressive student movement was also bolstered. We thought we had a cause to fall behind this leader. We participated in all protests (hartals) organized by Mujibur Rahman against the military. The conspiracy was instigated by Ayub Khan to discredit his opposition leader, Sheikh Mujibur Rahman and many other supporters including army personnel and civil servants. True or false, the case was never proven in the court of law, bolstering the movement against the army.[6]

In the end, the case weakened Ayub's presidency. Sheikh Mujibur Rahman made a bigger case to East Pakistanis against West Pakistan's discrimination in many areas. Since then, Mujib's six-point demand became his "mantra" of the East Pakistan federation movement supported by students with additional demands. The outcome was General Ayub

---

[6] Dr. Naazar Mahmood, "50 Years after Agartala Conspiracy Case," *Political Economy*, July 2018; "Textbook Incorrectly Describes Agartala Case: Shawkat," *The Daily Star*, June 12, 2010.

Khan had to resign handing over the power to General Yahya Khan. Yahya Khan, instead of easing the tension, added fuel to the fire leading to the Bangladeshi liberation movement when Sheikh Mujibur was denied the peaceful transfer of power to the newly elected parliament.

I would include here the interpretation of the story from a Hindu student perspective. The conspiracy theory was a brainchild of Ayub Khan in 1967. I did not believe the theory because Mujibur Rahman was not as progressive as other non-Muslim League leaders in East Pakistan. In addition, Mujibur Rahman was a political disciple of Huseyn Shaheed Suhrawardy. Mr. Suhrawardy, as prime minister of Bengal, was blamed for the communal disturbance in West Bengal in 1946 that qualified him to be the sixth prime minister of Pakistan (from 1956 to 1957). Despite all these charges, he proposed East Pakistan's autonomy (with East and West forming a federated state).

Students were more radical than Mujibur Rahman. Left politicians and students joined together to demand a federalism with passionate assertions of Bengali nationalism. All progressive students joined under the umbrella of a new Sarbadaliya Chatra Sangram Parisad (SCSP) or, in other words, a student resistance council demanding independent East Pakistan. On a regular basis, students organized protests with slogans like "Your Desh, My Desh, Bangla Desh, Bangla Desh." Since 1967 there was hardly any law and order in East Pakistan, at least in the student community, before Bangladesh was liberated in 1971.

Chapter 14

Mother's Worst Fear

As I was in the middle of all this chaos of career development, a letter came from my parents saying, "Do not worry. We are safe." It was alarming and confusing. I guessed they could not wish to write anything negative against the Islamist or military administration to jeopardize my life. I telephoned them and found out that my little sister had been kidnapped by several young Muslim boys. She was later forced to marry an older Muslim neighbor. There were two problems—my sister did not even finish her middle school, and the boy was not educated to our family's standard. It was a shaming event to the family prestige as well. My father sought legal action for a resolution because she was a minor. That irritated many Muslims. One day, they came in a group of over five hundred and surrounded our family, demanding they withdraw the legal fight. My father did not concede. That was when my parents wrote me the letter. My father's confidence and trust, along with his long-standing relationship with the community were shattered. He was shaken for fear of his own life, as well as our family life.

Unfortunately, the couple was hiding from public view. In the end, the girl was removed from the Muslim family and was put in a jail for trial in the mainland, Chittagong, away from the island. This cooled the atmosphere temporarily, but the tension remained during the entire legal fight. I was asked not to visit the family by friends. Instead, friends were helpful to the family to stay calm.

My father had a Muslim classmate and friend working for the Pakistani central intelligence branch (CIB). I befriended him in my first year of engineering college and used to visit him frequently at his residence in Dhaka. He would casually ask about the student movement in general terms, but we had no serious discussions on the matter. One day, I received a mail from the post office with a note from my father's classmate written on the envelop. "Come and see me," the note said. But it had been delivered by the general post office. That was the first time I suspected CIB was reading all mail and spying on students.

I was careful not to share anything political with my parents. My father's friend thought I may be innocent. A few days later, I met him. He knew more about my sister's case than my parents had told me. One good piece of advice he gave me at this critical family tragedy was, "Do not drag yourself in this mud of Hindu-Muslin fights; it is complex and lengthy, and your involvement will jeopardize your future."

My father also gave me similar advice. He knew my sister was in the Chittagong jail and offered his help to see her privately. My father and he had another common friend who was acting as Chittagong jail superintendent. I visited my sister in the jail, hoping to change her mind. She was totally brainwashed and was uttering all Islamic prayers to me. Within a three-month period, she had changed completely from praying to deities to pray to Allah. She was smart and intelligent. One could characterize the incident as a love story, but I doubted this was the case, as she was only fourteen years old.

The legal fights did not go well either. The medical officer who oversaw issuing a medical certificate of her puberty was totally biased. The medical officer was a disgrace to the profession, but as Hindus, we were at a loss. In the end, my parents had to swallow the pill of the pride and prestige. It was, of course, demoralizing for them. Anytime I visited them at home, I did not see them as cheerful and enthusiastic as they had been before.

I met my sister once more, after forty-two years, in 2014 when I last visited Bangladesh. She was still married to the same person and seemed happy with her life, children, and grandchildren. I wanted to reconcile but the intellectual and socioeconomic gap between my sister and me was too great. The society has evolved from the initial stigma, and my parents are not alive to suffer from that stigma.

My parents lost their lifelong confidence in the system of justice that was manipulated by the Pakistani administration—theirs was an incredibly sad experience of being a minority in a Muslim country.

Chapter 15

Meeting The Governor

Under normal circumstances, getting an invitation from the governor could've been a dream for many. Initially, I also thought so. Mr. Abdul Monem Khan (ML leader), not elected, was the Governor handpicked by then President, Mr. Ayub Khan. Ironically, it turned out to be a nightmare. In fact, it was not only nightmare but also the opportunity to have a clear understanding of the mindset of ML leaders and the military administrators. After all the episodes we'd already encountered, Hindu students were always in fear and tried to please their Muslim classmates and professors. They also worked exceptionally hard to impress professors in order to receive good grades in courses. On the top of that, I had the worst nightmare when I met East Pakistan's governor, Mr. Abdul Monem Khan.

It was pathetic for me because it was last year of my graduation in 1967. I was the student body's vice president (VP), and a request came from the highest office of the university for a handsome donation to Ayub's Arab War Relief Fund (AWRF) to help Arabs against Israel. It was the end of a month. Every month, we used to have a feast with a gourmet meal, cold drink, and cigarettes. The shopping was complete, except for drinks and cigarettes. I had to convince all the students to have the feast without those two items. Subodh Das, PhD, professor of civil engineering, was our hostel superintendent. I asked his advice. He recommended that we raised more funds so the donation from the Hindu hostel would look substantial. Professor Khabiruddin Mondal of civil engineering was the director of student's welfare (DSW). Funds from all hostels were raised under his overall leadership.

One day, all student VPs received an invitation from the DSW to attend a meeting with the governor. We were all thrilled without knowing what to expect. A military captain greeted us in the governor's mansion with snacks and tea, saying, "You guys are lucky to be treated by the governor like this. This rarely happens for anyone other than foreign delegates and VIPs." The rationale could have been the governor wanted to impress us to reduce the tension between engineering students and the administration.

The first shock came when the governor asked Professor Mondal, "Why don't you stop student unrest?"

The professor's response was simple, "There is not so much protest from the engineering university."

The follow up comment from the governor, "Why at all – small or large?"

Professor's answer was partially true because engineering students always had a rigorous course program, starting from the morning and extending till late afternoon with no break, six days a week. In contrast, Dhaka University students had much free time during the entire day. Engineering students would always work behind the scenes. For example, Jagannath Hall (Hindu students' residence) an epicenter of all students' movements. This would be our get-together center, where we would develop strategies and plan protests during nights and weekends.

The second shock came from another humiliating question. "Why don't you write Rabindra songs?"

The governor was referring to the inspiring literature and artistic creativity of the Bengali Nobel laureate celebrity (Rabindra Nath Tagore).

The professor was too dumbfounded to respond. There were no proper answers to the above questions. To justify himself, the governor switched his attack on minorities, especially Hindus. His point was Hindus had treated Muslims very badly during the British rule, and so they could not be the friends of Pakistan—a country for Muslims only. He forgot the history that Hindus had been under Muslim rule for over nine hundred years before the British took over. According to him, India should be treated as our number one enemy—a sentiment other Muslim League leaders had championed since the partition of Pakistan only for Muslims in 1947.

I was the only Hindu student leader in the delegate. The governor of a country is generally the protector of all citizens when it comes to any public display of biased views. This was a total humiliation in front of other classmates and the professor.

The governor's attitude or thought process was so crude it backfired on him, which was revealed by other students. Some of them could have similar feelings though. This was a firsthand direct experience of the mindset of Pakistani leaders, especially ML leaders. Till today, I could not find out if the governor knew of my presence. I was fuming inside and, at the same time, became fearful. I was not sure if I would get out of the mansion without being arrested with whatever false pretense might have been thought up, as the governor was surrounded by military officials. I did not react. Luckily, neither my fellow classmates nor the professor disclosed my identity.

That was when I promised to get out of the country for my higher education. But it was not that easy a challenge. Monem Khan remained loyal to President Ayub Khan till the end, though he did not have any popularity among East Pakistani Bengalis. He was replaced by Mirza Nurul Huda during the election protests and eventually assassinated by freedom fighters in October 1971.

Here is another anecdote from Mr. Monem Khan's governorship. The governor was once practicing law in the Mymensingh court. He encountered many prominent Hindu lawyers' pictures in the Mymensingh Bar Association building. The pictures irritated him. He visited the building after becoming the governor. He looked at the building and allocated government money to have it repainted. Under that pretense, all the pictures were removed and never put back—another story of Hindu hating. He was hailed by Muslim League for such a courageous act. But the process was very heinous.

Meeting the governor and having those discussion made me understand why minorities were so fearful and were migrating in large numbers at the earliest opportunities they could. For me, I wished for a better footing, rather than fleeing to India just to live a normal life.

Chapter 16

The Saga of Going Abroad

After graduating fifth in the class among all graduates in East Pakistan, I thought higher education would not be a problem in either the United States or Canada. With that goal in mind, I started applying to different universities. In parallel, I was also applying for different international scholarship programs available through the central Pakistani government process. The government process was advantageous to West Pakistani students because of proximity and preferential treatment. By the time the information reached East Pakistan, it was either too late or the deadline was over to complete the process.

Despite all those difficulties, I was successful in attaining a few scholarships. There were two other problems, though. I needed permission for a passport and permission to leave the country. There was much bureaucratic tape to untangle—obtaining police reports, clearing background checks by the village chairman, and so on. It was possible to get the passport bribing officers all the way. Permission to leave the country was a different hurdle (it required clearance from my employer). That was almost impossible to get one. It was a double-edged sword. The perception was you suffer. You cannot leave the country, and at the same time, you face social injustice while remaining loyal to the country against your will.

I made many attempts to get the permission I needed from the employer but was not successful. Permission was required to apply for a passport, and another layer of permission was needed to leave the country, even if you got foreign scholarships. I missed many such opportunities right after graduation in 1967. Finally, I decided to apply directly to universities for assistantship to avoid government bureaucracy. Even then, my attempts were not fruitful until Bangladesh was liberated.

My first attempt at the University of Ottawa before the liberation movement was such an example. A family friend, Dr. Bholanath Dey who was a practicing doctor in Saskatchewan, Canada, sent me an airline ticket; this was a requirement to get approval from the Pakistani government, as no foreign exchange would be given to those who were leaving the country on their own. Dr. Dey was disappointed when I returned his ticket because I could not travel due to the denial by the Pakistani government, who would not give me a permit to leave the country as an engineer. On the other hand, Muslim candidates, especially those from West Pakistan, would get government approval easily.

Chapter 17

Toxic Political Environment And Observation

The Bangladesh civil war had been brewing since the inception of Pakistan in 1947. Language, culture differences, the Bengali language movement, lack of leadership of Muslim League (ML) party, the power struggle between leaders, wild dreams of reestablishing the Ottoman Empire, and artificial inflation of Hindu-Muslim tension by military rulers all attributed to the 1971 civil war. The final blow for the revolution came after the landslide election win by Sheikh Mujibur Rahman (Mujib) in 1969 for a democratic government and adamant refusal by the military to transfer power to the civilian administration. Another secondary leader, Mr. Zulfikar Ali Bhutto of Pakistan People's Party (PPP) emerged among different confusions prevailing in the country, claiming a theory of a fictitious and fake second majority from West Pakistan. What a joke to conspire with the West Pakistani military.

Many nations did not rate Bangladeshi atrocities as disastrous as was deserved, even though there were tremendous human casualties—three million dead, ten million refugees, thousands of rape victims, and many thousands of children born out of rape. The world never knew many individual stories of those who faced premature death. I was one of those ten million refugees. Ninety thousand Pakistani military personnel were involved in killing, looting, and raping with the help of local hooligans or Muslim League supporters also called Razakars, Al-Badr, and radical Islamists (Hindu haters and Anti-Indians). All ninety thousand soldiers responsible for Bangladesh massacres, including their generals, were captured by freedom fighters with the help of the Indian Army. India was not economically strong enough to punish those soldiers or powerful enough to fight US interests in Pakistan. Each soldier and the leader were released by Pakistan, receiving no penalty. Even the ruthless generals (like A. A. K. Niazi and others) went free without punishment and had a lifelong agenda of revenge against India. Neither international politics nor the newly created country, which, with its people not totally united, and was helpless on this account could be of any help. India could have pursued International Criminal Court (ICC) type justice if it had enough resources.

Unprecedented cordial relationship and cooperation between Hindus and Muslims on the ground, especially among Mujib supporters were observed during nine months of the liberation fight. I thought a new era had been reached and was encouraged about the future of the liberated secular country, which I thought was worthy of my sacrifice. Sheikh Mujib's release from Pakistani jail in 1972 gave an additional boost to this grandiose relationship and good feeling. But unfortunately, the honeymoon was short-lived (lasting from 1972 to 1975), and Sheikh Mujibur Rahman was assassinated. His assassination was devastating for many of us who sacrificed their lives and had a great future hope in him.

More devastating was the turning of the Muslim-Hindu relation to the worst from 1975 to 2008, when the Bangladesh military coup took over the administration. The Hindu-Muslim relationship fell back to the same level as it had been during the Pakistan military regime. Deep-rooted religious hostility and religious policies adopted by the dictatorial administration of Ziaur Rahman (Bengali Army General) flared up in Bangladesh. Who knew Bangladeshi minorities would face exactly similar religious discrimination at the hand of a man who had fought to liberate Bangladesh? Major Ziaur Rahman was the major (Bengali high official) defecting from the Pakistani army to declare over the radio for a secular and democratic constitution in an Islamic country. Eventually after President Major Zia's assassination, it became worse in next two administrations including one during his wife, and Prime Minister Khaleda Zia before democracy was, again, restored by the current prime minister, Sheikh Hasina.

Accurate documentation of some events is important, and that is my motivation for writing this book. My narratives will shed many lights on what minority families living in a Muslim country, especially one that is a military dictatorship faced. Such living and survival may be characterized as a curse. Though *Six Months and Six Days* describes my survival story in the civil war of East Pakistan and now Bangladesh, it reflects similar stories of many who may not be as fortunate as I am to be able to tell their stories. This is the story of Amalendu Chatterjee, a survivor, who grew up in a Muslim country (Pakistan) and went through life-disrupting and life-threatening experiences but still was able to build a new and successful life in Canada and then in the United States.

Looking back, I see the ideal of our struggle—to root the four pillars in Bangladesh—could not have been preserved. There could have been many reasons. I can cite two or three important ones. The first one was the assassination of the founding father. The second one was the pardoning of all the radical Islamist who were against our struggle for democracy. The third was the power struggle after the assassination and the corruption and chaos at the highest levels of the administration.

Chapter 18

Damned At The Dam

In hindsight, I realize that the decision to transfer to Kaptai Engineering Academy had one good outcome. I was able to attain admission to the University of Ottawa. But permission to get out of the country was impossible. I missed the first session starting in September 1970 and then January 1971. Further extension could have been possible, but government logistics were hard to predict. I almost gave up. Then came the military genocide. Then came most crucial time of my life's decision during the military crackdowns—stay at the job or flee?

I had some breathing time to think it over and over while at Kaptai. I had another colleague, Tapan Das, who was one year senior to me, from Bangladesh University of Engineering and Technology (BUET). He was the first to abandon his post. It was easier for him because he was from the countryside of Chittagong—a few hours from Kaptai by road. I could not decide that easily. I was too worried for the family, with no contact, no exchange of mail, and no telephone calls for many months even before the military operation. Kaptai was safe for a few weeks, as it was far from military activities with access by only one road. The military was busy fighting to take control of other big cities. But I knew they would be coming to Kaptai any day. There were two reasons they would come—(1) to save the Kaptai Dam, which was vital for the electric grid connection and (2) too many Biharis (100 percent military supporters and India/Hindu haters) were killed by Bengali liberation fighters. None of those initial fighters was Hindu in the liberation group at that time and at that place, Kaptai.

One night, news broke out that Bengalis, in collaboration with the Bengali Regiment, which revolted from the Pakistani army, had killed the Bihari chief engineer, along with all his family members and dumped them over the dam. Major Ziaur Rahman, who revolted from the Pakistani military at the early stage of freedom fighting and who later became president of Bangladesh was directly or indirectly involved in such atrocities. I shivered with fear. There was no way to escape punishment by the military for the killing of a high-ranking officer and his family members who happened to be non-Bengalis. Presumptions were these non-Bengali officers would ever support the Bangladesh freedom fight. I was convinced we all, especially Hindu employees, would pay the penalty for it for no fault of their own. I was the only Hindu officer left on the project.

Initially, I was hesitant to discuss my decision with other Muslim colleagues. An opportunity came along while I was talking to our chief engineer of the Engineering Academy, Emdad Ali (a Bengali). He was originally from West Bengal and was ready to flee because he could not tolerate killings of the innocent and the loss of basic human rights. His decision emboldened me to share the idea with other members of the Kaptai project. This only happened because Mr. Ali could confide in me, being the only minority officer, his thoughts about brutal murders of the innocent. Close to ten families agreed to flee with us. Of course, no Bihari family would join us. They were waiting for the military to show up to revenge the mass killing of their friends and colleagues. An unfortunate part of civil war is that citizens of one ethnic group are killing other citizens of a different ethnic group. Of course, the army was the instigator of the kind of environment that existed then.

Mr. Shamsuddin, the power station manager and his direct report Mr. Saleh, executive engineer, decided not to join us. They tried their best to stop the massacre of the Biharis, but they could not save them all. Mr. Saleh's daughter lives in North Carolina. Mr. Saleh visited his daughter, Ms. Tasneem Saleh Lopa, and came to see me. He told me, in his own words, that he and Mr. Shamsuddin were rounded up by the military in a death squad due to misreporting by some of the Biharis who survived. Mr. Shamsuddin was killed instantaneously. Mr. Saleh survived by luck. Both had good intentions, but it was difficult to sort out all the details in the chaos. They were too naive to understand that the military would not spare anybody, given so much killing was going on everywhere.

Many of us were convinced the military would hunt everybody who killed the Biharis. Major Ziaur Rahman, an officer of the Bengal Regiment, was one of them. His first stop was in Kaptai after the radio broadcast of Mujib's message of independence on Kalurghat radio station. Being a military officer, he knew he had to develop strong resistance against the military. Trust had been lost completely between the Bengali army units and the West Pakistani army units. When Major Zia entered Kaptai, he eliminated small army units mostly staffed by Biharis originally for the security of the Kaptai Dam. Other Bengalis who were workers at the dam were instigated by Zia to kill civilian Biharis. No Bengali Hindu officer was involved in killing of Biharis to my knowledge. Major Zia was a sensation for the freedom fight during the early stage of the revolt against Pakistan. Nobody with sound mind could have survived the initial thrust of the military when they entered any place of strategic importance or any important city. For a Hindu officer to stay back in Kaptai and face the military was an invitation for instant death. Killing Biharis was bad. Hindu officers (though they were not responsible) had little chance of passing military scrutiny. Major Zia later became the President of Bangladesh, a military dictator, after the assassination of Mujibur Rahman, who initiated revival Islamism in the constitution.

I sheltered and protected two Bihari families in my own residence for months, hoping sheltered families would show some compassion or empathy. I even stored food for months before I left so they didn't have to go out to face Bengali hooligans. Contrary to my trust, when I arrived after the liberation, my residence had been looted, and my personal belongings had been burnt, as if I'd never existed. Those two families repatriated to West Pakistan at their earliest chance with the cooperation and help of the army. To my understanding, this was an award in exchange for secret information they shared with the army about Kaptai Dam.

In hindsight, I realized asking for a transfer to Kaptai Engineering Academy was a blessing. My posting at the Academy from 1970 to 1971 gave me an unexpected opening for an experience when Bengali liberation fighters started killing non-Bengali employees of the Academy – a life-death situations with physical torture by one ethnic group to the other during the liberation movement after the early period of crackdowns by the Pakistani military. If I had stayed back at the Barisal site, my situation could have been as dangerous as well, given there was less civility among fieldworkers. The dilemma of keeping personal moral and ethics intact became harder at the power line construction site. I could not yield to the pressure of the contractor to sacrifice the quality of the work to increase his profits. I wanted to compromise with him on the necessary volume of work (a small design change) for more profits at sites with boiling sand. It was not convincing to him, and he wanted to maximize his profits in any corrupt way he could.

I asked for cooperation from higher authority, and it was not coming. I got the impression the higher authority may have already been compromised. The longer I stayed at such a job, the worse it would get. And that was why I asked for a transfer. I knew the contractor would help my transfer and get someone of his choices to replace me. My gut feeling worked. The transfer happened quickly because of the contractor's ministry level connection. There were constant conflicts, including fistfights between my subordinates and the contractor's employees. These fights would erupt for two reasons—cash pay-offs and the honesty of a few subordinates.

One day, there was bloodbath. One of the contractor's employee was gravely wounded, with broken ribs and a wound to his head that was bleeding. He was hospitalized, and police had to be called. The contractor settled the case outside the court with a large payoff to his employee, as well as my subordinates. To my mind, nothing was fair. I felt bad and miserable because I tried to be honest, so the quality of work did not suffer. Unfortunately, I could not get it through the corrupt military administration from top to bottom.

Early in my professional career, I met many officers while performing my jobs as an engineer. Some of them kept their social distance, but some became remarkably close, and I socialized with them beyond office norms. Mr. Enayet Karim, the nephew of A. K. Fazlul Huq, was one of them, though he was a follower of ML with friendly gestures out of his vested interests. Mr. Karim kept my friendship for a long time. But during the freedom war, he did an about-face. Construction contractors become friends for their vested interests. They could never become real friends—a lesson I learned at the early stage of my professional life. If their money interests were not met, they did not hesitate to stab you in the back.

Initially, I did not pay much attention to those details. I slowly learned many tricks during this crisis. I matured while serving the cause of humanity—saving human lives. As a byproduct, I also realized the influence of climate and education. I was reflecting on the fact that educational instinct had led me up to this stage of survival and on other causes motivating people to help each other. I talk of climate because many of us lived on vegetables and fruits naturally grown in those areas during the daytime. The other part was, had I not planned my journey to leave the hilly tract of Kaptai Academy, where would I have been? You become your own mentor during crisis.

Chapter 19

Packing For The Road

Where to go and how to pack was quite a dilemma. Besides, none of us had extra money to travel. But the consensus was we must leave the dam to avoid revenge by the army against some of us. There were so many rumors and so much misinformation the army could never make an unbiased judgment at the spur of the moment. Our chief engineer was able to convince the local bank at Kaptai to distribute a meager amount of money against our overdue salaries. Emdad Ali, the chief engineer, decided to cross over to India via Demagiri in Mizoram province, India. Mr. Ali had family in West Bengal and could survive there for a few months. West Bengal is a Bangladesh neighboring province in India in the west, and Mizoram is a province in the neighboring Chittagong Hill Tract of Bangladesh. River Karnafuli originates in Mizoram and flows through Bangladesh before it reaches Bay of Bengal. Mr. Ali also had a teenage girl of his own, whose safety was his top priority.

Most of my other colleagues decided to go to their respective home in different parts of Bangladesh. Mr. Emdad Ali, in my opinion, made the right decision. He did not have an ancestral home in Bangladesh village like many of us. He had a house in Dhaka, but going to Dhaka would have been a nightmare with a family of four, when there was no civilian transportation available. Being a Muslim, Mr. Ali could have gotten permission from the military for travel, but that was also risky because of the Kaptai massacres.

By Kaptai massacres, I mean first the killing of the Biharis before the army could take over control of the Kaptai Dam and then the killing of the Bengalis by the Pakistani army in collaboration with the surviving Biharis as revenge. History may never have been written correctly to blame Major Ziaur Rahman, who became president of Bangladesh after the assassination of Sheikh Mujibur Rahman, as the cause of both atrocities. There were no minorities in power to orchestrate anything of such a large scale at the Kaptai site. It was a fight between Bihari Muslims, who were strong military supporters, and Bangladeshi Muslims, who were AL supporters. Let me emphasize that no property was looted by freedom fighters. They knew keeping morale high was a prerequisite under such circumstances to achieving the bigger goal of freedom. Freedom fighters, of course, had to kill Biharis so they could not regroup to kill Bengalis after the military took over.

Mr. Ali decided to cross the Indian border using the channel opened for army operations. I could have followed the chief engineer to be a refugee in India. Like Mr. Ali, my family came first in my thoughts. On the second thought, after sensing the military operation surrounding the Chittagong seaport, I did not want to be trapped on the island. The seaport was completely under the control of West Pakistan's navy. It was also not safe for any private transportation in the Bay of Bengal. Chittagong port and its surroundings were vital for the army for any intruder attacking the navy. It was also vital as a cargo port, with shipments arriving from West Pakistan for the repletion of the military's arms and ammunition. As a result, entry to the island was impossible.

I could have taken a risk and tried to go to the island anyway. But even then, once you were on the island, you may be in a deathtrap— stuck between other opposing forces, such as radical Islamists or social miscreants like the Razakars, Al-Badr, or other Islamists, in addition to the army. My second thought was to stay away from the family so we did not all face the same peril at the same time and at the same place.

I started with a small bag (with pants and shirts), a camera, a notebook, and a small amount of cash. Before I left, I helped to hide two Bihari families in my residence on humanitarian grounds, hoping they would save my personal belongings. Despite all of the radio news, mostly from the BBC and Akashvani (Kolkata) in favor of the liberation, I was convinced the army would win, and we would be back to normalcy as usual; that had happened many times before—protest, unrest, army torture and killing for a while, and then normalcy under stricter army administration.

I entered the world of uncertainty in the mid-week, April 1971. I was ready in my mind to face any adverse situation, but I thought I would capture every moment with my camera and the notebook as I moved around. When my attempt to go home failed, I watched the movement of the army and freedom fighters as I was moving away from the direct route to Kaptai from the Chittagong army cantonment. My goal was to stay away from the direct route, but I saw the army movement. I was happy to take pictures of skirmishes between ordinary citizens and the army as the public was putting resistance in the army's way—roadblocks formed by trees and bricks. There were dead bodies of those killed by the army on the way and dysfunctional tanks on the road. It was scary and exciting to join forces against the army. Those pictures were not the instant pictures of today. they were captured on rolls of film, which I lost as I moved place to place, with no belonging at the end when I entered India as a refugee after six months of struggle.

I needed a footing to initiate my next move. I met thousands of people who were in the same boat as I was. They were helping each other. It was like a large, instant cooperating system. Nobody had any normal life. Everybody shared what they had with others. People opened their homes to stranger like me to sleep or take a shower, irrespective of any ethnicity or religion. If that were an indication of a free country, we saw all the elements of what a new country would look like—a true democracy for all, with no religious discriminations. But unfortunately, the reality has turned out to be completely different today.

My curiosity was to survey what was happening across the country. I started moving place to place mostly on foot, by rickshaw, or boat to cross creeks or rivers (though I often swam or walked through knee-deep water). The mode of the freedom operation was to make a random hit against the army and then run away and hide. The army would never venture out at night. Rather, soldiers would return to their camps in the city after a daylong operation in the suburban areas.

In the initial stage of the army's crackdown after March 25, 1971, freedom fighters, along with the Bengali officers who had revolted from the Pakistani-controlled cantonment, launched random attacks on the strongholds and well-organized camps of the Pakistani army with all its army gear. There was not enough time for those freedom fighters to be trained well or equipped for formal war. They were mostly asked to fight and take shelter at the Indian border.

I saw many reminiscences of struggles on my way as I wandered around. I soon realized such uncoordinated attacks with no long-term strategy could not be a winning strategy. Moreover, such randomness caused more danger for innocent civilians. During the daytime, the well-organized army would go out in remote areas to burn out houses and kill innocent people in a line-up—a genocide of extreme measures. One random attack on the army would cause thousands of houses to be burnt and many thousands of revenge killings. The army soon realized every Bengali could be a freedom fighter or every house could be the hiding place of a freedom fighter.

Fortunately, freedom fighters would provide cover against the Pakistani army while refugees (children, women, and the elderly) were fleeing to the Indian border. I did not want to join such random groups as those I met on the way. I wanted to be part of the struggle in my own way—as part of an organized operation.

Chapter 20

Bhutto's Manipulation

Mujibur Rahman, the founding father of Bangladesh, was not initially a trusted leader by Hindus. Mr. Rahman was a strong follower of Hussain Shaheed Suhrawardy, the chief minister of undivided Bengal (from 1946 to 1947) during the British rule. Mr. Suhrawardy was not a popular chief minister because he had been explicitly accused of having an indifferent attitude to incite violence like Hindu slaughters in Kolkata in 1946. The Agartala Conspiracy was a framed charge as an Indian agent to sabotage Ayub's regime. It was brought by Ayub Khan against Mujibur Rahman. Z. A. Bhutto also played a role in it, though Ayub Khan did not like Mr. Bhutto. Such political dynamics started changing Hindus' support for Mujib. I was also leery of Mujibur Rahman at the beginning of the language movement.

During the 1971 liberation movement, when Mujib combined his six-point demand with progressive students' eleven-point demand into one consolidated demand of nine points, he got my full support, as well the support of many other progressive minority students. Over the years, 100 percent of Hindus trusted and supported Mujibur Rahman during the movement, while fewer than half of Muslims, so-called Islamists, and Biharis supported him for the Bangladesh liberation. That was the grudge the Pakistani military had in all those nine months of the movement to hunt down minorities, mostly Hindus, in all corners of the country. During our initial hideout and struggle in the jungles of Barisal, it was not known whether Mujib was alive or whether he had been killed by the army. We guessed Mujib could have been arrested and flown to West Pakistan. This guess was proven to be right.

On the other hand, the theory of the Pakistan People's Party (PPP) leader Z. A. Bhutto—the Two Majority Theory—worked well to break up Pakistan. Mr. Bhutto conspired first with Ayub during the Agartala Conspiracy and then with Yahya Khan after Mujib's landslide victory in the democratic election. Mr. Bhutto manipulated the army General Yahya Khan to resign and took over the presidency of Pakistan in 1972. Mr. Bhutto started his political career as the foreign minister during President Muhammad Ayub Khan's administration. Mr. Bhutto resigned his post as foreign minister and formed his own political party, the PPP. Both leaders were opposing Ayub's administration. But Mr. Bhutto was the master manipulator. On the one hand, he opposed Ayub Khan, but on the other, he also opposed Mujib's six-point demand for East Pakistan's autonomy. Ayub Khan wanted to negotiate with Mujibur Rahman, but Bhutto raised public opinion in West Pakistan against Mujib's six-point demand.

Mr. Bhutto was an extremely manipulative politician, who discredited Ayub Khan for power. Bhutto fully exploited both the controversial win of the 1965 election over Ms. Fatima Jinnah and the loss of the war against India in the same year, working to reverse Ayub Khan's popularity. There was an assassination attempt on Ayub's life while he was visiting Dhaka in 1968. In addition, there were widespread protests against Ayub Khan with derogatory chants in both East and West Pakistan. President Ayub Khan also had a heart attack during that period and became paralyzed, forcing him to resign.

He resigned but without a peaceful transfer of power to a civilian government. He invited his trusted general, Yahya Khan, to take over the control of Pakistan, fearing political prosecution by a civilian government. Again, Mr. Bhutto started his manipulating game, now with General Yahya Khan, and forced him to declare the election in 1970. Mr. Bhutto hoped to gain a majority win to curb Mujib's rise. When Mujib achieved the absolute majority, he manipulated Yahya Khan with two unpopular theories. First one was Mr. Bhutto won the majority votes in West Pakistan. The second one was Mujib could not be trusted by West Pakistanis, and Pakistan would be destroyed under Mujib's leadership. Yahya tried to negotiate a compromise between Bhutto and Mujib but failed. The result was the start of the 1971 genocide by the West Pakistani military in East Pakistan.

Chapter 21

Fleeing To India

In the middle of September, we, a group of forty to fifty, decided to head toward the Indian border with help from freedom fighters, who were crossing the border frequently. I decided to go to India because displaced people were also fleeing to India on their own. They thought being refugees in India would be better than the hell in Bangladesh villages. Nobody knew where the next meal was coming from if it came at all. Nobody liked the constant movement from place to place or the lack of places to sleep either, though the movement was necessary for individual security and safety. They thought the refugee camps would have better facilities and, under Indian management, would have at least some sort of guarantee of international standards with financial aids.

I did not flee alone, abandoning the group. I took my group with vulnerable families with me and made sure those who did not wish to flee were taken care of. I could have stayed back but decided to explore what was happening on the other side of the border after almost six months of struggle to survive. Of course, it was the same motivation others had. We found an escape route that involved trips by foot, boat, and rickshaw. It took us ten to twelve days to reach the Jessore border. It was not easy to sustain the long days. We were under constant threat from the army. We had to travel at night only. All refugees crossing the border formed a human chain and moved forward only when it was signaled safe by Mukti Bahini. Mukti Bahini was the name of the freedom fighters in Bengali. Initially, it meant all Bangladeshi fighters, including teachers, students, peasants, and government officials, all those who left the city in fear for their lives and took up arms against the army.

Then proxy soldiers from the Indian Army joined the mix. In the end, it was an Indian military operation. These Mukti Bahini were controlling the India-Bangladesh border. The Pakistani army did not dare go to the border at night. We had to sleep under trees. We had no change of clothes, no shower. But village people were ready to help us with drinking water and food. Villagers, both adults and children, lined up to help us one to one. They were mostly Muslims but supportive of the liberation movement—the opposite of Islamists who aided the military to massacre Hindus.

It was a sigh of relief when we crossed the border and boarded a train to Kolkata (Shialdah). People were hugging and kissing the train itself, the ticket checker, and the station. Local people from West Bengal showed full sympathy, offering help and knowing who we were by our fatigued appearances. It was a scene of being born again with new life and new freedom.

From there, everybody was on their own. Some went to the refugee camp, and some joined their families. I went to my sister's place (Hindmotor, Hoogly). Hindmotor was an industrial city close to Kolkata. This was the first time I'd changed my clothes in almost six months. It was such a sigh of relief. I felt like a dead man walking. But my worries for parents continued, as it was not possible for a word from them to reach me. I had to spend another three months until the liberation wondering if they were all alive.

All employees of the government in exile (in India) had to get permission to go back to Bangladesh from India. I left for Sandwip first in January 1972 after the liberation. The moment my parents and I saw each other was like a second birth as well. There was constant hugging, kissing, and questions and answers, as if we'd found our loved ones from heaven. It was impossible to be out of each other's sight for a moment as long as I was on the island. It was also time to ponder what I had done and what I needed to do next. I could stay back in India and become Indian citizen. I could come back with Bangladesh government to be a Bangladeshi citizen and join the previous employment. I decided the latter to pursue some dreams of the childhood. It was really a proud moment to be the citizen of free Bangladesh after so much sacrifice.

Chapter 22

My Identity Crisis

I was born in 1944 while India was one country. The British divided the country, and I first became Pakistani not by my choice but because the territory I lived in happened to be part of Pakistan. This arbitrary partition, with no option of repatriation for East Pakistani minorities to India, created an identity crisis for many. It was further reinforced by constant discrimination against, bias toward, and even hatred of our community as a foreign agent. At times, my safety and security, as well as that of my family, was raising the question of our real identity— Indian, or Pakistani? I participated in the Bangladesh revolution to identify myself as Bangladeshi. That also became questionable after the assassination of the founding father. I realized my own identity crisis when I started understanding politics, religions, and ethnic prosecution first by the Pakistani military junta and then by the Bangladeshi junta. My family became refugees in India after 1978 and then became Indian. I came to Canada in 1972. Now, I, personally, am not recognized by either Bangladesh or India though I married an Indian girl. 'Six Months and Six Days' is a story of struggles for the right to be Bangladeshi.

My identity or the identity of my family being in a minority group always came under question because of discriminatory policies imposed by the Pakistani military. I felt like a foreigner in my own country. And also the minorities in Pakistan were treated as if they were Indian agents. Overcoming this identity crisis was troubling and frustrating at times. There was so much hatred for Hindus and India in East Pakistan that I did not know where I belonged, India or Pakistan. Minorities were totally marginalized in Pakistan. They were treated as second class citizens with little rights because they were not Muslims.

My two parents were polar opposites on this issue. My father was always blindsided by his profession, and my mother was obsessed with her children's future. She wanted to leave Pakistan, but my father loved his country and the people he served. Another reason for his resistance was he was not sure if he could maintain the same lifestyle as a refugee in India with nine children as he enjoyed on the island.

You generally fall in love with a country you are born in or grow up with. But I was confused. Why? Religious, political, and ethnic discrimination was so harsh you were feeling it every day. Love for the country was always in question. Revolution for Bangladeshi freedom and its intimate participation gave me a renewed sense of identification. Our inspiration came from the spirit and principle of Indian leader Netaji Subhash Chandra Bose, who started an armed revolution against British rule. Netaji formed the Indian National Army (INA) for his struggle and formed a government in exile in collaboration with Germany and Japan. Netaji was an Indian administrative service (IAS) officer trained by the British. He concluded, in his mind, the slow negotiation initiated by the Indian Congress Party and promoted by Nehru and Gandhi would not do the job. That was why he became a hero in the minds of many Bangladeshi freedom fighters or guerrilla fighters.

All these efforts were learning experiences for Bangladesh's freedom fighters and the Bangladeshi government in exile. The only difference was that Bangladesh was successful, but Netaji's efforts failed due to his untimely death or capture. Two Japanese executives of Fujitsu Network Switching, the company I worked for, came to my residence for a dinner and were very proud of Netaji Bose. I was feeling proud again to relate to a completely new identity, which I fought for myself, rather than being born with. My dream of freeing a country was a prize for all my family members. My children would have been proud of my achievement as well if they had been born at that time. My grownup children born in Canada pushed for the memoir of the Bangladesh event and my involvement. That is an incentive for this book – to narrate the half-baked story of an almost achievable dream. It is half baked because real freedom didn't last long. And I, or my family, was searching again for a new identification. My mother and other siblings migrated to India in 1978 and became Indian citizens. I was looking for a bigger identification with more freedom and flexibility. I became a Canadian citizen. Again, that was a fulfillment of my own. Later, for a better economic and professional life, I became a US citizen. With such a paradigm change, I became a citizen of the world, having less restriction of travel and other financial and social benefits. Such benefits helped me to sponsor two of my younger siblings to come to Canada and the United States. They enjoy the personal freedom they could never get either in Bangladesh or in India.

There is one message of this section. Netaji Bose's INA lost the war, and his whereabouts are still a mystery. If Pakistan would have won against the freedom fight, many freedom fighters, including Sheikh Mujibur Rahman, could have vanished from the earth much earlier. But unfortunately, it happened few years later after the independence and the history had been rewritten after Mujib's assassination.

It crossed my mind many times to quit during the struggle. I did not expect another struggle would start for minorities after the assassination of the founding father. But looking at the history and examples of great men who sacrificed their lives for a greater cause kept me going and kept others who followed me going. Yes, there was always doubt in my mind as to whether we could keep going with high spirits. The positive attitude toward liberation we saw in people was remarkable. Little did we know such phenomena would change overnight when the founding father was assassinated. Civil war, or the liberation war, was the ultimate tool we had to use after we'd tried peaceful protest and democratic election for the peaceful transfer of power. The commonsense approach didn't work with the army. In the beginning, I thought it would be over soon. That "soon" never came. I started counting hours and days. As each day passed, I was falling into a trap of confusion and uncertainty.

A country had just been born. Everyone was trying to establish his or her importance in the country. That included freedom fighters, as well as Pakistani supporters. There was violent disruption to settle the difference and score points. The result was the assassination of the leader. We all had been following the dream of the leader—a secular and progressive democracy away from Islamic domination. With the leader gone, the nation's dream died prematurely. Islamic domination grew stronger and stronger by the day. Minorities started feeling disappointed and started leaving the country because it was the same environment minorities had faced under the Pakistani regime. What a sad part of human psychology that people so often lose sense in the face of power or money!

Back at Hindmotor, my brother-in-law bought some pants and shirts for me. The next day, I went to Mujib Nagar, India and met Mr. Emdad Ali, the chief engineer of the Kaptai Academy. He asked me to register. He also asked me to work there with token remuneration. I agreed. I went to see my maternal aunt from Barisal, who had fled earlier and was living with her daughter on 10 Galif Street in North Kolkata. She insisted that I live with her daughter, son-in-law, and grandchildren. She asked me if it would be OK to guide the school-going grandchildren. Her son-in-law (Hamendra Lal Chatterjee) was a physics professor at the city college and an examiner of the secondary high school final exam. It was an opportunity, indeed, to be in touch with the home environment I had missed for so many months. I also had a chance to work with professor, Chatterjee to grade the final examination of 1971 high school students.

I started commuting either by bus or on foot from Galif Street to No. 8 Theater Road (so-called Mujib Nagar). This was also the time of the Naxal movement in West Bengal. I would occasionally hear gunshots at night on my way back from the office to the residence. It did not bother me that much initially because I was used to it while inside the Bangladesh territory.

One day, an army Jeep showed up early morning at the doorsteps of the professor's quarters. They were asking for me. All the neighbors were scared and thought the professor was in danger. Nobody would go out to talk to the lieutenant cornel sitting in the Jeep. I dared to go out. The cornel was cordial and introduced himself as Colonel Bora and asked me to accompany him to his office. His mission was to collect all intelligence of Bangladeshi power lines from me in case they would engage in a sabotage to disrupt the power supply in Bangladesh. It was gratifying for me to be of some use during the crisis of the movement. Pakistan surrendered before such activities were needed. I met Colonel Bora as a military attaché once at the Indian embassy in Bangladesh before leaving for Canada. I never had any other contact with him afterwards. Many years later I met one gentleman, Mr. Shyamal Kumar Mallik in North Carolina. He came to visit his daughter, Madhulavi Majumdar (our friend) in North Carolina. Mr. Mallik was an intelligent officer and was advising Indira Gandhi on Bangladesh related intelligence. He was also posted in Bangladesh as military attaché to the Indian embassy. We had many interesting discussions about the liberation of Bangladesh and interactions he had with Bangladeshi leaders including Sheikh Hasina.

In addition, Professor Chatterjee was well connected with the ruling Indian Congress Party. He helped me get a travel document for international travel through his political connection, though I did not have to use it because Bangladesh was recognized by many countries, including Canada, my country of future interest, within a few months of liberation. Going to the United States for education was not my first choice because of America's policies toward Pakistan selling arms and ammunitions. Eventually, however, I would end up in the United States for economic and climatic reasons. My wife did not like the rough, cold weather of Canada.

Chapter 23

The Liberation

The Bangladesh liberation war can be viewed from various angles. The war did not start as a liberation war and went through many historical transformations. Different experts have scrutinized this liberation based on their own perceptions. Chronological details could not have been recorded correctly due to constant dynamic changes within the social and political environment. So I believe some memoirs like mine would play a valuable historical role. The final scrutiny of the liberation was bastardized by the same people who fought against the liberation. I along with many others had been observing it in an unconventional but analytical, factual way. I did not know all those official facts, but field observation served as evidence to confirm the official position. The bottom line was freedom could have been denied on two grounds. Pakistan had the arms to kill more Bangladeshis. Prolonging the duration of the war for many more months while the mediation was sought by international bodies like Pakistan did in Kashmir could have saved Pakistan from the humiliating defeat. India's smart move put an end to that possibility, and the war ended in only thirteen days after India got involved on the western front. All credits go to Prime Minister Indira Gandhi for not going to UNO for arbitration as his father, Mr. Nehru did on Kashmir creating a scope of never ending disputes between two countries. Indira Gandhi's smart move also proved to be an utter failure of the Nixon-Kissinger foreign policy on Pakistan which Mr. Kissinger acknowledged later.

Chapter 24

Operation Chengiz Khan
And Name Calling

We were getting weary in the trenches. Normal life was already tough but was getting tougher daily, while high-level, barbarous politics highlighted no real picture of the human tragedy. Big powers with their vested interests played maneuvering games as if this were a chess game and those involved were pawns to be moved about. In addition, both President Nixon and Secretary of State Henry Kissinger made personal and vulgar attacks, calling Indira Gandhi a "bitch," a "witch," and an "unattractive woman." Such remarks against a state head by powerful leaders had never been heard in history.

These were, of course, private remarks, declassified later, but rumors went viral. It started with two polarizing forces in action during the cold war of the Nixon-Kissinger administration. President Nixon thought he must preemptively defuse the Russia-China relationship during the cold war so that USA enjoys both relationships in USA's favor. One way to do was to initiate a favorable trade relation with China. Pakistan had a good relationship with China during the cold war. The United States wanted to take an advantage of the strategy with a personal connection with the then Pakistan's President, Yahya Khan. All these diplomatic moves were going on when the Pakistani military started its operation of human massacres in Bangladesh. India wanted to pre-empt Pakistan on the world's stage on refugees that fled East Pakistan to West Bengal, India. Simultaneously, India's other mission was to support the freedom fighters fighting against Pakistan and weaken Pakistan on the eastern front. Russian help was essential for India. In the end, India, with

Indira Gandhi's shrewd leadership, won the fight for the recognition of Bangladesh as an independent country. Even Kissinger wrote in his book later, 'Mrs. Gandhi was a strong personality relentlessly pursuing India's national interest with single mindedness and finesse. I respected her strength even when her policies were hurtful to our national interests.'

The cost was high though. Mrs. Gandhi lost US support in her diplomacy, including PL 480 aid. It did not matter in the end. China also aligned with the United States against the Bangladeshi fight. Knowing how it worked out may be a lesson for all of us. I must admit I was too naive to understand during the time it happened how Indira Gandhi outwitted Nixon diplomacy. In summary, the Nixon-Kissinger foreign policy was very raw and unsophisticated. No other past president after Nixon kept any proper lid over the China policy, and that is why China, with its autocracy, became the fastest growing economy and a powerful military force with modern war machinery. The world would pay a heavy price due to China's nuclear power. Added to that is the Russia-China-Pakistan axis that could revive the old cold war, bringing instability in the world because all of them have nuclear power. Bangladesh, with its manpower, proper democracy, and economic growth could play a vital role in South Asia and Southeast Asia. It would need great political leadership, and I see that missing in the current Bangladesh political environment.

During our freedom war against Pakistan, we heard two buzz phrases constantly—the "US Seventh Fleet" and "Russian Cruisers and Destroyers Armed with Nuclear Warheads." And the two were facing each other near the coast of the Bay of Bengal. A few months after Pakistan's Operation Searchlight on the eastern front of India, Pakistan was losing its grip on the East Pakistan territory. Bangladesh freedom fighters, with the help of the Indian Army, were gaining ground to defeat Pakistani soldiers. It became evident that the war would be decided on behalf of the freedom fighters, and India would declare war on the eastern front.

Finding no other alternative path toward winning, Pakistan declared an operation, Chengiz Khan, on the west front on December 3, 1971.

In parallel, Pakistan was also asking the United States for help and military material support in order to kill innocent people. As diplomacy with China was one of the top of priorities for the Nixon presidency, the United States started diplomatic initiatives, as well as making physical threats by showing the presence of the Seventh Fleet in the Bay of Bengal. In terms of diplomacy, the United States first tried a UN-sponsored cease-fire like the one in 1947 when Pakistan attacked Kashmir. When that attempt failed, and US intelligence reported an offensive attack by India on the western front, the United States dispatched its Seventh Fleet into the Bay of Bengal.

The same day, Indira Gandhi addressed a mass gathering in the West Bengal racecourse. I attended the gathering and was overwhelmed with what she had to say. On the way back to Delhi, she declared war against Pakistan and against operation Chengiz Khan. The war was won in thirteen days. How did Indira Gandhi outsmart all US moves? Indira Gandhi did not fall into the UN trap as her father, Mr. Nehru, did in 1947 during the Kashmir dispute. She preplanned everything the day refugees started flowing from Bangladesh to India. All intelligence reports suggested that Pakistan was most vulnerable when Yahya Khan had been manipulated by Z. A. Bhutto, the leader of the PPP, not to transfer power to a civilian government, even with a landslide victory of a fair election by Mujibur Rahman. Bhutto's words were, "Rahman cannot be trusted for the interest of Pakistan." Such insinuation infuriated Bangladeshis and the Awami League party. Things got out of hand when the Pakistani army started cracking down on innocent people in big cities of East Pakistan, and a revolution started.

The crackdowns spread from big cities to small cities and then villages, especially against minorities. East Pakistanis mostly Mujib's supporters started fleeing the country to India. The Pakistani army adjusted, now cracking down in the border areas, scaring fleeing innocents. India sheltered these refugees. The number of refugees increased, and freedom fighters were launching random attacks against the Pakistani army. The strategy was not effective. India started giving the freedom fighters organizational support, along with arms and ammunitions. The Indian Army concluded that the Pakistani strategy to control East Pakistan was getting weaker and weaker because of the organized pressure from the freedom fighter. Indira Gandhi was looking for this opportunity to play a diplomatic role in her own way—unlike her father, Mr. Nehru, not depending on the UN. In early August, she signed a twenty-year treaty with the USSR. In addition, a few countries recognized Bangladesh unofficially even before it was liberated.

As part of this treaty, the USSR dispatched cruisers and destroyers equipped with submarines right after the US Seventh Fleet made its move. With USSR under her belt, she started a six-nation tour, including to the United States of America. Highlights of her mission were to get support from other UN nations. Japan, Canada, the United Kingdom, and some other countries agreed to provide refugee aid, but China and the United States showed little support. The United States proposed a UN-backed resolution to help the Mukti Bahini. Indira Gandhi rejected that proposal outright and the USSR vetoed the resolution—a right strategy to win the third Indo-Pakistan war. Nixon-Kissinger could not take such defeat by an Indian woman leader, and it was in this context that Nixon-Kissinger made those unfortunate humiliating, derogatory, and shaming remarks on Indira Gandhi.

Those moments were unforgettable for all of us freedom fighters. In the end, it took the United States and China many years to recognize Bangladesh after the country's liberation, along with many other UN member countries. Bangladesh also became a bona fide UN country member.

A Protest, Not A Liberation War.

A protest started against the Pakistani military for expressing various grievances, including the failure to restore a civilian government. Protests were so intensified that Ayub Khan had to resign by transferring power to the next general, Yahya Khan. Yahya Khan promised a fair election, and Mujibur Rahman won the election. Mujibur Rahman was an East Pakistani Awami League (AL) political leader. West Pakistani political leaders, especially the leaders of the Pakistan People's Party (PPP) could not trust East Pakistani political leaders and always undermined their abilities to lead the country. PPP conspired with the military not to hand over power to the majority winner, further angering Mujibur Rahman and his supporters. Anger, unrest, and protests reached the stage of a complete nonfunctioning of the government administration, more so in East Pakistan than in West Pakistan. There were some sporadic protests in some parts of West Pakistan in support of East Pakistanis, but the protests in the west weren't as widespread or as strong as those in the east.

The Ugly Face Surfaced

Yahya Khan had made consolatory statements, suggesting he was listening to East Pakistani grievances during taking over the power as chief martial law administrator from Ayub Khan. He declared a general election for the country but did not realize the result would be polarized. He also did not realize PPP's leader, Z. A. Bhutto, would be emerging as a competing and manipulating leader from West Pakistan. Ethnic sympathy and Bhutto's influence played a role and Yahya Khan was reluctant to hand over the power to Mujibur Rahman. By ethnic sympathy, I mean language and culture were dominating factors, rather than the religion. In the eye of West Pakistani leaders, East Pakistanis were inferior Muslims, considering most of them had been converted from Hinduism. West Pakistani political leaders, including the military had the impression that East Pakistanis did not speak Urdu, and so they could not be at par with West Pakistanis. This bias was also reflected in West Pakistani authorities' hiring practice of civil servants and military personnel—a full-scale discrimination on all fronts, though the population of West Pakistan was less than that of East Pakistan. West Pakistanis were able to do this because they had the governing power. It was sad part of the Pakistani military complex—those who held the reins were totally blindfolded by the machinery of power, with no patriotic thought of the country and its citizens. Holding the land was the primary concern, and its people were secondary.

Operation Searchlight

The situation that existed in 1970 and during the early part of 1971 went beyond the government's control as I recall. There were many agonizing dialogues among many civilian leaders as reported by military leaders in the news media we saw. Many of us were convinced a peaceful transfer would happen out of such intense dialogue, but then the world saw the ugly face of the Pakistani military. Pakistan decided on the night of March 25, 1971, to engage in mass killing and arrests of intellectuals, students, Hindus, government officials, renowned professors and left-leaning politicians. We observed that the military thought these limited atrocities would scare everyone, and the unrest would stop.

When the military failed to squall or curb the Bengali nationalist movement and people started taking up an armed resistance, the Pakistani military raised to a full-scale military operation, giving it a secret military code name, Operation Searchlight. The brutal and ruthless military operation was unknown to the public initially. Operation Searchlight was planned in January 1971, almost three months earlier than the infamous day in the Bangladeshi calendar, March 25, 1971. General Tikka Khan, also known as "the Butcher of Baluchistan," was given charge of the East Pakistan operation for his experience of atrocities in another province of Pakistan, Baluchistan.

Under Tikka Khan's leadership, arms and West Pakistani military personnel in plain clothes were secretly shipped to East Pakistan. All the while, in parallel, fake dialogue between Mujib, Bhutto, and Yahya about a negotiation to settle the power transfer was going on in public. In fact, it was a public facade—a cover under which the West Pakistani army was getting fully equipped to initiate brutal killings of and atrocities against Bangladeshis including Bengali armed and police forces.

The military power could not even trust Bengali armies and police forces, and full preparation was going on to run the operation unilaterally with West Pakistan forces only, as if East Pakistani Bengalis did not belong to Pakistan. A statement by Tikka Khan made his position on East Pakistan Bengalis clear, "I do not need people, just the soil." These words were recorded in a diary by Major General Rao Farman Ali, who served under Tikka Khan as per the West Pakistani army commission's report conducted after the liberation.

Operation Jackpot

Operation Jackpot was the code name given by the freedom fighters and the Indian Army's combined operation to counter Operation Searchlight. Tikka Khan failed measurably in his initial operation against the resistance given by sporadic Bangladeshi freedom fighters. It was disappointing for the West Pakistani army leaders, of course. Slowly, army leaders were desperate to find a real butcher harsher than Tikka Khan. Lieutenant General Tikka Khan was replaced by Lieutenant General A. A. K. Niazi, another butcher and human rights violator. He was chosen because he volunteered to take over the command of East Pakistan operation in April 1971. Prior to his volunteering, many other distinguished Pakistani generals such as Lieutenant General Bahadur Sher Khan refused to serve in East Pakistan to kill people.

West Pakistan's plan for Operation Searchlight was to capture all cities in a matter of days by killing and torturing as many people as possible. They also planned to take control of the border and the police force in that short period. They started worrying, as the liberation resistance became powerful. As the resistance endured for days and then weeks and then months, the army started worrying. Their face in the world was exposed as ugly and uglier. Slowly, it became more and more difficult to keep its internal affairs internal as the brutal pictures of dead bodies lying on the street proliferated.

On the other hand, the freedom fighters were also getting worried. The strategy of armed resistance with no organization was failing to hold cities they'd captured initially. They also became desperate and were seeking the Indian Army's help. Finally, that help arrived in the form of code name Operation Jackpot. The objective of Operation Jackpot was to attack Pakistani forces using three key strategies to weaken the West Pakistan Army and demoralize army personnel. Freedom fighters demobilized the Pakistani naval operation, let refugees cross safely to India, and crippled Pakistani attacks on all borders.

It worked. The final blow came after the declaration of war by India against a preemptive attack by Pakistani forces on the Indian west border. The success story of Operation Jackpot was that it forced the surrender of more than ninety thousand Pakistani soldiers, along with all its commanding officers on December 16, 1971—the largest force to ever surrender since World War II. It was so disastrous that even generals could not fly out with army jets in any neighboring country.

Reaction By World Bodies

It was sad to observe that there was no unanimous support of the Bangladeshi freedom fight by all countries, including the United Nations Organization (UNO). The United States of America and China, two security council members, objected to Russia and India's efforts— a partisan phenomenon of international politics. But Indian Prime Minister Indira Gandhi made a very successful campaign before and after the war to get the support of key countries, including forcing Bangladesh to be a member country in the UN, despite some opposition by the United States and China. Iran and the Arab world, including Sri Lanka, were not great fans of the new liberated country. Iran and the Arab World did not support Bangladesh because they opposed the breakup of Islamic countries. Sri Lanka did not offer its support because Indian dominance in the area was not in Sri Lanka's long-term interests due to constant conflict between the two countries.

Eventually, a country was born, with all its diplomatic relations with all UN-recognized countries.

India's Inaction Enforcing Secular Constitution

The war confirmed a big victory for India. It also confirmed the birth of a new country, Bangladesh. But India faced many challenges in terms of ongoing foreign relation. I was not that much worried about relations the

United states and other Western and European countries. I was worried about restoring the relationship with Pakistan. I was also worried about the ongoing relationship between Bangladesh and India.

India failed in both areas. There was the so-called "Simla Agreement" (also spelled "Shimla Agreement") with Pakistan after the creation of Bangladesh. Z. A. Bhutto fooled India again with a diplomatic negotiation by signing the agreement on the dotted lines but not signing on to the commitment to abide by the line of control (LOC) on Kashmir and to restore a normal socioeconomic and political relationship. More than 50 percent of the Bangladeshi population did not have a good perception of Indian support for the liberation of the country. India showed indifference in both areas. Pakistan increased its terrorist activities with little repercussion, and Bangladesh became more radically Islamist and even killed its founding father. India did not have the proper foresight with an innovative and aggressive plan. India thought Bangladesh would be adjuvant after India had sacrificed so much of its resources and army personnel—a total miscalculation and error in judgment.

The liberation movement started instantly after March 25, 1971. It had spread sporadically and quickly all-over East Pakistan. The outcome was doubtful in everybody's mind from the beginning. Bangladeshis had seen similar killings before and knew it would be squashed very soon by the army. The army had its playbook on hand. Military leaders knew East Pakistani Muslims could be brainwashed in the name of religion. Blaming India and Hindus for East Pakistan's misfortune could also work miracles. Pakistan played Islamic trump cards in conjunction with other Middle Eastern countries for over two generations with the hope of misdirecting East Pakistan's future. Most youths grown up with that culture had difficulties realizing what was happening during the movement. That was the reason of poisonous Islamic atmosphere flaring up again a short period after the liberation.

———

No East Pakistani Muslim, not even Sheikh Mujibur Rahman himself, or his party wanted to separate from West Pakistan. It was never in their plan or in their blood due to blind faith of religion. Even in Mujib's party, there were strong Islamist leaders. Hatred of minorities was so ingrained in their brains that they would rather be subordinate to their Muslim brothers of West Pakistan rather than living in a free cosmopolitan country of their own in East Pakistan. West Pakistani's brutality, torture, and killing of intellectuals and progressive politicians changed the landscape when many had to hide or take shelter in India. Unorganized freedom fighters popped up in many cities out of anger irrespective of party affiliation except Biharis and Islamists. Even then, the expectation was that, after a few days (as with previous episodes), the situation would be under control. Things started changing when a provisional Bangladeshi government in exile, with all AL supporters, was formed and full cabinet positions were announced somewhere in the border area. It could have been in April 1971 with headquarters at No. 8 Theater Road, central Kolkata.

Despite such bold steps by some AL leaders, some cabinet ministers were skeptical and thought such a move could embolden their negotiating or bargaining powers with Pakistan. In one famous example, Khondaker Mostaq Ahmed was designated foreign minister. Mr. Ahmed played dubious roles during the freedom fight as well as after the assassination of Sheikh Mujibur Rahman. Of course, he was overshadowed by other leaders of independent Bangladesh. The government in exile had a wild dream of independence with no resources or organizing abilities. They did not even have organized military power to streamline different sporadic uprising of resistance against the well-organized Pakistan Army, with full support of the US government.

The Bangladesh government in exile had to surrender to the Indian government for all logistical support in managing the refugee flow, as well as organizing resistance inside Bangladesh to weaken the morale of the strong Pakistan Army, with ground, navy, and air forces greater than ninety thousand strong. It was frustrating for most of the population who were not directly involved. Many did not have any direct access to different sources to know the international politics at play. Many Pakistani supporters depended on the government-sponsored news media. The result was confusing as far as the real progress by the freedom fighters. Freedom fighters wanted immediate actions by Indian forces. India wanted its own terms, both from Bangladesh and from Pakistan.

India had to develop a shrewd but winning strategy. Slowly, the Indian government became very vocal, along with actively supporting the freedom fighters—sending military aid and raising the issue of refugees with the international bodies. In addition, there was constant harassment of the Pakistan Army by freedom fighters as soon as they left their barracks to go to the suburban areas. It got under the nerves of the Pakistani military, and they decided to launch a preemptive air strike against the Indian Air Force on the western border to divert Indian pressure in Bangladesh. It backfired on the Pakistani forces, giving India the opportunity to declare a full-scale war on December 3, 1971. India knew it had some international support because of the influx of refugees. The unprovoked attack by Pakistan on the western sector of India was an excuse for other Western countries, except the United States, to provide needed aid to refugees and moral support against military invasion. The USSR was one such example. Even before the full-scale war, Bangladeshis saw a retreat of Pakistani forces to their barracks. No Pakistani fighter jets were seen flying in the sky, and the same was true of speedboats, which stayed in their ports rather than going out to patrol the sea and river ports.

Propaganda machines of India via radio and BBC broadcast reinforced people's mindset. They thought the human suffering would be coming to an end soon. But how soon was the question on everybody's mind. Every time a Pakistan Air Force (PAF) plane was downed by the Indian Air Force (IAF), there would be joy you could hear from a distance. We knew India was recognizing Bangladesh but did not expect a declaration of war with the recognition of the country. Many people put December 3 in their calendar to assess the days of the defeat of Pakistan. Nobody expected it would come by December 16, 1971—so soon.

Soldiers Surrendering And Spectacular TV Show

We concluded Pakistan was fighting a demoralized war; there was no way to win such a war. When all Pakistani soldiers in East Pakistan—more than ninety thousand—lined up to surrender, it was broadcast over TVs/Radios. It was the largest surrender of fighting forces since World War II. People walked miles to locations where public or private TVs/Radios were available. It should be noted that TV was not available in every house as of today. All the freedom fighters were dancing in the street when they observed all the Pakistani officers of all divisions (army, navy, and air) laying down their arms. Pakistan paid some penalties—shaming one-third of their armed forces of all divisions, army, air force, and navy, by bowing to their main rival, India, and losing more than half of its population to a new country.

But Pakistani news media was playing a different tune, saying the Muslim world was against India partitioning a Muslim country into two pieces, and India would pay the price. It was also interesting to listen to the statement some officers, especially General Jamshed and Brigadier Siddiqi, made in response to reporters' questions. According to them, it was part of a game; you lose some, and you win some. What a sarcastic comment to make when referring to the lives of human being—a game played with the lives of millions of innocent people.

India, on the other hand, was playing with a dangerous and fiery situation. Close to thirty thousand active freedom fighters wanted to kill each one of those Pakistani soldiers. Before the surrender, Pakistani soldiers were mad at freedom fighters and were circulating a false fatwa in the battlefield, stating that those Muslim freedom fighters were Hindus, and raping and killing them would not be against the religion. India was careful enough to observe the Geneva convention and took care of the well-being of every soldier captured. Bangladesh wanted at least all high-ranked officers, close to two thousand or three thousand, to be punished by international tribune. Again, India fell victim to Bhutto's manipulation in the Simla or Shimla Agreement and did not take any action, rather entrusting Pakistan to dole out internal discipline.

According to the pact, India agreed to return all soldiers. Bhutto agreed on the dotted line but never followed through on his end of the bargain—which was to abide by the line of control jurisdiction decided by the UN for the Kashmir dispute and to punish some officers listed by Bangladesh for the Bangladeshi massacres. Again, it was an irony. All Biharis who had actively participated in the atrocities and looting were repatriated to Pakistan with no consequence for their heinous actions against their fellow human beings in Bangladesh. Unfortunately, India, also at the end, could not maintain a trust of majority Bangladeshis due to unforeseen religious, business greed and other socio-political dynamic.

Part IV

Chapter 25

Efforts Going Abroad

Crossing the border and taking shelter in India were not the end of my life's struggle. I tried to arrange a travel document to travel to Canada while working with the intelligence branch of the Indian Army. I got one international travel document after several months of work with Indian politicians. In hindsight, I see that a citizen-less travel document obtained from the Indian government while I was a refugee in India was a better choice for going abroad. I had not thought Bangladesh would administer the process, in its formation, the same way as Pakistan did. Initially, Bangladesh followed all administrative protocols left behind by Pakistan because all previous bureaucrats took over the administration. One of the provisions was that no engineer would be allowed to leave the country. As a result, I had to hide my identity as an engineer in order to leave the country even after the liberation.

It was so surprising that the entire Pakistani Armed Forces, with all its air and naval power numbering more than ninety thousand, had to surrender in thirteen days. Nobody expected that the war would end so soon. Complex international politics played a role beyond our expectation. But nine months was a long time for the Pakistan Army to sustain the war. Indira Gandhi's excellent political maneuvering, including Indian Army's strategy to block the movement of Pakistan's army with the help of Bangladeshi freedom fighters, played a winning role.

In addition, the army got tired of killing, and their support infrastructure was crumbling because supply routes were blocked by India all around—air and sea. Even internal river ports of Chittagong,

Dhaka, and Khulna were blocked by freedom fighters. It was so joyful for me to make another try to go abroad from Bangladesh—a free country, the creation of our efforts and the sacrifice of many. I tried three different passports and three different addresses, of course, with bribes just to avoid the bureaucratic loopholes of the chaotic administration. The country was free, but the old bureaucracy was still in place.

I tried to travel using the citizenship-less travel document issued by the Indian government while I was a refugee. But the Canadian government asked me to wait for a visa because they were in the process of officially recognizing Bangladesh. Canada was, in fact, the third country to recognize Bangladesh after India and the USSR.

I had the right as a freedom fighter to demand what I wanted. With that right, I could have pushed my case harder with the Bangladesh administration. But I did not wish to expose myself too much, knowing fully well that there were many Islamic influences in the administration. Moreover, I could not attach myself too much to Bangladesh because I had a different dream. I also took the high road. If all freedom fighters become selfish about achieving their own goals, the country would be in chaos, and along with it, the bigger goal of creating a country for all who fought for it and who did not fight for it—Nelson Mandela's great philosophy.

My first attempt to get the approval of the Bangladeshi government to travel abroad failed because my passport had the professional title of an engineer. I reapplied immediately for a second passport with a different address and different profession (just a science graduate). I did not want to miss my last chance to come to Canada in fall 1972. It was embarrassing to ask for so many extensions. My admission letter indicated admission for a Master of Science degree, and that helped me to get the government approval. Even then, I was not sure whether I would face trouble in customs at the airport. Sure enough, customs asked for my undergraduate degree certificates. I told the officers my belongings had been looted and our house burnt during the genocide of minorities. That helped my case. What a relief! I was scared it would be an ugly scene if my identity as an engineer was revealed.

I arrived at the Ottawa Airport in late September in the middle of heavy snow with no foreign exchange in my pocket. I would ever remain grateful to my friend, Dr. Delip Das, who paid for my flight to Canada. Unfortunately, my hero died of kidney failure. Delip had a roaring medical practice in Bangladesh but had to flee Bangladesh, leaving his practice when jealous Islamists attacked him only because he was a successful Hindu doctor competing with Muslim doctors. Luckily, he was able to start a similar practice in a suburban area of West Bengal.

At the Ottawa Airport, there was a student welcoming booth. Students at the booth arranged my transportation to the foreign student temporary dorm. Then a pen pal, Haripada Dhar, PhD, who wanted to help me in Ottawa upon arrival, met me in the dorm and provided some temporary financial support. He was from a Bangladesh minority community and knew from personal experience that my financial situation would not be solvent. It was a new start but a hard one. I was late by a month for the academic session. I was also out of touch with any research at the university level courses since my graduation in 1967.

The next day, I met my graduate studies supervisor, Professor Georganas. He was cordial and welcoming. He recommended that I not take a full load of courses, just to recover from the trauma I had gone through. He also knew $2500 a year assistantship would not cover all my expenses. He recommended I be an immigrant so he could help me with other financial aid. He pointed to a building (the immigration office), which could be seen from his third-floor office. He was also sympathetic when I appeared before him with my left arm wrapped with a cast.

I slept in the international dorm on an iron cot, blanket, and pillow. After a week, we moved to a room shared by many international students, along with one Canadian. It was snowing the night before I was ready to meet my advisor. The Canadian friend invited us to go out to see the snow at night. I was excited to venture out because I'd never seen snow before. It was fun to stay out for a few hours. Unfortunately, I was not properly dressed against cold winter; my ears and fingers were almost frozen when we returned. I didn't have winter boots either. The next morning as I was heading to see the advisor at the department of electrical engineering, I fell. The steps were frozen, and I didn't know the dangers of a harsh winter. My left arm was twisted. I had to go to the doctor before I could see the advisor.

Following the advice of the professor, I went to the immigration office the next day and applied for an immigration card. The paper arrived at my address within a week after fulfilling the requirement. It was so easy then.

I remember I was taking a course (State Space Techniques) offered by Professor Desouza. It was basically a course on solving nonlinear differential equations. There, I met a gentleman from the Russian embassy. He became very friendly with me. It was either because I was from Bangladesh or because I was one of the smartest students in the class. He started asking many questions about the Bangladeshi civil war. He even invited me for dinner a couple of times. It was a treat for me because I did not have the luxury of eating out. After the session was over, I met him once or twice, and then he disappeared. Nobody would return my call anymore. His real name was unknown, but he went by as Alexander. He was a real mystery. The other classmates thought he joined the class thinking the course would offer some techniques related to space exploration, which was hot at that time in 1970.

I finished my Master of Science degree in systems engineering in two years, having published many articles in technical journals and qualified to continue my PhD with a National Research Council (NRC) scholarship in 1974, which was around $12,000 a year. What a jump from $2,500. In economic measures of that time, it was more than enough for a single person. I saved money to buy a secondhand car (a Renault) even after supporting my family in India and Bangladesh. This purchase was a miracle for a person who'd never seen a car before he was eighteen years old. I was now driving one.

Selection of PhD topics was critical to pass the qualifying exam. My supervisor, Professor Georganas, was as ambitious as me because I was his first student to the program. Computer communication based on

DARPA (Defense Advanced Research Projects Agency) was the broad subject he chose for a research topic, which was intriguing, and I spent over a year taking different courses.

During the process, I came across many interesting topics under investigation by famous scientists in the field (Dr. Kleinrock from the Internet Hall of Fame, Larry Roberts, and others). They all worked on ARPANET (Advanced Research Projects Agency Network), the first digital computer communications network. My research topic was, Congestion Control in a Computer Communications Network – innovating an efficient algorithm for connecting high speed computers for sharing research data. I finished my thesis and PhD in three years (from 1974 to 1977).

Finally, I got the job I had been looking for all those years—in the field of telecommunications. I started working for Bell Canada to plan the first packet switched network separate from a telephone network, only for data communications. It was called DATAPAC, the first packet switched X.25 equivalent digital data network—the brainchild of a technical group in Bell Canada guided by Pramode K. Verma, now a professor emeritus, University of Oklahoma.

Chapter 26

A Secret Trip After Forty-Two Years

I made a trip to Sandwip in 2014 with my older son, Avik Chatterjee, MD, MPH. Avik was the most adventurous member of our family to take the trip. My wife, Arundhati Chatterjee, MD, was scared to travel to an Islamic Bangladesh after listening to my stories of the harrowing six months I'd endured there. My other son, Ayan Chatterjee, MD, MSEd, was doing his residency. I dared to take this trip after Sheikh Hasina came into power. Even then, I had to take extra precautions to plan all our movements while in Bangladesh with a network of friends who were in high positions in the government. They took care of our stay and travel to avoid any adverse situations.

All my family members, except the baby sister who was forcibly married to a Muslim boy, had relocated to different parts of the world now. One brother lives in Canada. Two of us (my baby brother and I) live in the United States. One sister lives in India. My eldest brother died, but his family lives in India.

I'd had opportunities to visit Bangladesh before, But my father, in his lifetime, warned me not to visit Bangladesh in the middle of the turmoil of Bangladesh's politics and social discrimination. Ayan and my wife were not as adventurous as Avik. They did not accompany the two of us.

On my last visit to my ancestral home with Avik in 2014, I found the pristine landscape was missing. Many homestead, including our ancestral graveyard, had been swallowed by the sea or occupied by Muslim neighbors. Concrete roads and houses had been constructed, and mechanized transportation had been introduced. People drove cars (which I had never seen in my childhood). Dockyards had been built. You never got wet while boarding ships or speedboats. You could cross the Bay of Bengal in fifteen to twenty minutes, instead of the four hours it took in the early days to reach the mainland. The most miraculous change was the change of the sea's course, eroding in one side of the Island and forming landfill on the other side. Sea came closure to my ancestral home and one can see waves having a landfall a few yards from our ancestral home.

Most noticeable was the influence of Arabic and Urdu on the Bengali culture of Bangladesh, especially among Hindus. The contrast or the difference could be felt when you spoke to a Hindu Bengali in West Bengal versus a Hindu Bengali in Bangladesh.

As for a claim of ancestral properties, it has become impossible. At least two generations of Muslim families have settled in the property. Official document or records have been changed or altered. Nobody knows you—"out of sight, out of mind." The government will not cooperate because they depend on electoral votes of those who reside in the place, not outsiders like me. Even a slight hint about reclamation will ignite Hindu-Muslim tension and trauma. I wondered if the tranquility of Hindu-Muslim unity and coexistence I saw after the disaster of cyclone and tidal waves would ever come back (my father's influence).

It was a visit that could've been enjoyable for both my son and my parents if they were alive in our ancestral home. My mother saw both my sons, Avik and Ayan. But my father never saw either of them, as he died in 1978 in Bangladesh before our sons were born in Canada. My mother died in 1997 in India. My father arranged a big party when my older brother's children visited the ancestral home from Kolkata. It was a party of seventy-five to a hundred people. All meals were cooked at home in the backyard. Even the fish were caught in the backyard pond. This was the story my nephews and nieces narrated during my wedding ceremony in Kolkata in 1977. My visit to the ancestral home with Avik was totally secretive, arranged by my friends. I never knew what to expect if someone could identify us. There was no law and order in the village, and random killings of foreigners were the norm. Moreover, there could have been some grudge held by neighbors, as I had been in favor of the liberation, supporting Mujibur Rahman and opposing the ML administration and Yahya Khan.

I was incredibly careful in planning the trip so my son and I would not face the fate of Mr. Abhijit Roy, a Bangladeshi American blogger who was hacked to death many years later by radical Islamists while returning from a book fair. Memories of my parents being attacked by local Islamists during my sister's forceful conversion to Islam on the island and my father's warning not to visit Bangladesh during his ill health haunted me throughout my short trip of seven to eight days in 2014.

Many years later, one of my middle school classmates, Mr. Rezaun, contacted me in Durham, North Carolina, out of the blue. He wanted to see me and my family. He'd spent years tracking down my whereabouts. He knew I'd left Bangladesh many years back. Through some common Muslim friends, he'd traced me in North Carolina. He came with his one son and his family, three grandchildren, one summer afternoon 2018. From various discussions, I suspected Rezaun's son was a current Islamist supporter, though he was not born at the time of the freedom fight. Rezaun did not graduate from middle school and had no clue what his son and I discussed. I could not understand the purpose of his visit, after almost forty-six years. We were as graceful as possible to entertain them.

In the middle of their short stay, they upset my wife when they were preparing for Islamic prayer using our bathroom and carpet without asking our permission. She was upset because she thought it would have been a common courtesy for people who'd lived in the Western society so many years to ask for permission. They showed their religious aggressiveness, an audacity. Later I found out that Rezaun had been among the mob of five hundred people attacking my family in Sandwip during my baby sister's kidnapping. Rezaun's daughter-in-law and her children were part of an Islamic school and madrassa somewhere in Chicago. Rezaun sponsored all his other children and grandchildren to immigrate to the United States and boasted they all—some ten or fifteen of them—worked or went to a madrassa or Islamic school in Chicago. Rezaun called me many times since then, but I was not excited to maintain any contact, as there was nothing intellectual or challenging between us. Moreover, they lived in an Islamic ghetto and had not graduated to an assimilated lifestyle of the United States of America.

In a short summary, Pakistan's trajectory since 1947 reveals many wrongdoings, including brainwashing two generations of young children. Violations of human rights came under question many times before the Bangladeshi war. Who knew a powerful nation like the United States could ignore such violations due to vested interests based on national security? This phenomenon became difficult to swallow when light was shed on it many years after the Bangladesh genocide.

While in a Bangladeshi village trench escaping Pakistani military genocide in the cities, I did not have much idea about the United Nations Organization (UNO) and international politics for peace and justice for common people. We were fighting for justice and the democratic right of people and thought the UNO should also fight for justice and peace. I knew Russia and the United States were on the opposite side of the war. Russia and its allies joined India and the Bangladeshi fighters. That was a sore spot for the Nixon-Kissinger administration, I perceived. Their reasons were love for dictatorial power and the ability to control people and their hatred for so-called socialism and communism. The United States and its allies joined Pakistan to punish India and Russia. In addition, Nixon wanted to separate two communist powers—China and Russia. That was an ideological partnership on the world stage.

I never thought it could stoop to a personal level among political leaders. Nixon and Kissinger's praise for Pakistani leaders and people contrasted with their shaming of India's leader and people, especially women. It did not make sense then and does not make any sense now. Indians and Pakistanis contain the same or similar genes. Unfortunately, no UNO organization can resolve such animosities at a personal level. It defies human norms and the civility of individual leaders.

The Nixon-Kissinger conspiracy against India was revealed later in many declassified documents[7]. Where was the slogan of democracy by Nixon administration then? What I'm saying is that poor countries cannot get justice from powerful countries or international organizations that purportedly promote peace and justice because of veto powers exercised by powerful nations. As evidence, George Bush attacked a dictatorial but peaceful country, Iraq, on the false grounds that Iraq was responsible for the 9/11 attack and that the attack would bring democracy to replace Saddam Hussein. Weapons of Mass Destruction (WMD) were never found. No Iraqi was a participant in the 9/11 attack. Rather, many Saudis and Pakistanis were involved. But those two countries received royal treatment because this suited the safety and security of the so-called United States of America.

The Nixon-Kissinger administration committed crimes. The then US ambassador, Mr. A. Blood, tried to persuade the US administration not to support Pakistan. But he was sidestepped. A war reporter, Joe Galloway, narrated this episode in Mr. Blood's obituary. Characteristics of war crimes included supplying weapons for the killing of innocent civilians and children, raping women, destruction of property, and looting assets. The UN and other organization were as ineffective then as they are today for Ukraine. The veto power of the UN security council, with five powerful members, does not serve the purpose it was formed for—keeping peace or avoiding the illegal occupation of territories against people's will. I strongly felt the mandate of the UN could have been for the people, not for military dictators or vested interests of powerful nations.

After the independence of Bangladesh, we all thought the time of radical Islamism at least in Bangladesh had diminished. It was joyful for a few years for all communities. It was a forgone conclusion by Bengali intellectuals that the Pakistani Islamists went into hibernation. Another theory was that Bangladesh, under the influence of progressive force, secular democracy, and

---

[7] India News: Declassified Tape: How US "Saved West Pakistan" As India Liberated Bangladesh and 'The Terrible Cost of Presidential Racism' by Gary J. Bass, NYT, September 3, 2020.

advancement of science and education would find contradiction with Islam. Unfortunately, we were so wrong. The Nixon-Kissinger conspiracy played a role before the war or even after the war by the new administration giving legitimacy to organized Islamic political parties. Some believe, though I do not have any proof, that the US Central Intelligence Agency (CIA) helped to revive religion in Bangladesh to discredit India and Russia. Islamists were smart enough to roll out a propaganda that Islam or Quranic science was the forerunner of all science advancements. More mosques and Islamic schools were built during the insurgence period (1975 to 2008) or even after that. Such phenomena have reached to a stage beyond control, with funding from all rich Islamic countries. Due to Islamic propaganda, marginalized citizens did not receive the ownership of the country. That was the reason for the second wave of minority massacre in Bangladesh. Bangladeshis under Islamic and military rule played the same Islamic/Pakistani tone of Hindu/India hatred as I heard during my childhood before the liberation. They borrowed the same playbook from Pakistan.

The warning is for those who claimed offense at the following observation, made in this history of Bangladesh since its inception: What Bangladesh has lost—to be painfully accurate, what Islamists have been trashing in pursuit of power and chaos for marginalizing minorities—is the willingness and ability to share a common identity irrespective of religion. It would seem to be self-evident truth. But people may not agree. Good news is as Leonard Pitts in his opinion, in Google news said, 'Not everything that is faced can be changed, but nothing can be changed until it is faced.'

Worldwide, many Samaritans like me living outside Bangladesh have the liberty to influence Bangladeshi policies and encourage them not to follow Pakistan's path. There is no lack of organizational efforts, but lack of resources hampers the progress.

Support Of Terrorism in Bangladesh

Bangladesh revolted against Pakistan and succeeded. The initial result showed some promise for Bangladesh but reverted to the same situation as existed during the Pakistani regime after the death of Sheikh Mujibur

Rahman. Different players were enacted. Instead of the West Pakistani military, it was the Bangladeshi military. The Bangladeshi military was, again, controlled by Islamic radicals and Muslim League supporters.

A change to the 1972 Bangladeshi constitution, with Islamization, minority discrimination, hatred for Hindus and India rose to the same level as it was during Pakistani regime. There remain hard-core Islamists in Bangladesh, indoctrinated by the Pakistani military for two generations (from 1947 to 1971). They were silent during the liberation movement and during the short period of Sheikh Mujibur Rahman's administration (till his assassination). They resurfaced with a stronger desire for vengeance, fueled by the next three administrations—those of Major Ziaur Rahman, Hussain Muhammad Ershad, and Khaleda Zia of the Bangladesh National Party (BNP) (from 1975 to 2008)—brainwashing another two generations of Islamists. The root of such uprise rested on strong Pakistani supporters (civilian and military) who Sheikh Mujibur Rahman pardoned after the liberation. These politicians and Islamists had been borrowing from the same playbook Pakistan used before the liberation. That is the challenge Sheikh Hasina has been facing in the attempt to turn the country into a real democracy.

Chapter 27

Changes In Bangladesh's National Identity

Bangladesh was once very proud of Hindu culture and Bengali literature of Kazi Nazrul Islam, novel laureate Rabindra Nath Tagore, and many others. Regrettably, much of that is disappearing. The idealism of Bangladesh, irrespective of religions and ethnicity, has slowly lost its steam. Islamism was introduced in school textbooks, replacing many verses of great authors, poets, philosophers, and novelists with Urdu words. One can notice the remarkable difference if one talks to a Bangladeshi Hindu and a Hindu from West Bengal. The Islamists of Bangladesh were already changing the very identity of the Bangladeshis from a linguistic one, based on which Bangladesh was created, into a Bangladeshi Islamic one. They have practically destroyed secular democracy in Bangladesh, while Major General Ziaur Rahman of BNP started the process of Islamization. Lt. General Ershad of the Jatiya Party declared Islam as the state religion in 1988, and then the currently ruling Awami League government reaffirmed it through the 15th Amendment to the constitution in indelible ink, by using its two-thirds majority in the parliament. All three parties have done it to appease the Islamists.

By using their sway on the present government, their clerics are publicly denigrating religious and ethnic minorities. Common Muslims were encouraged to grab minority-owned properties, including graveyards. The government purged the textbooks of non-Muslim authors and introduced language into fifth grade Islamic religious textbook stating that non-Muslims are akin to animals.

Working at a micro level, they have been Arabizing the culture. They are replacing Persian borrowed words with Arabic words. For example, "namaj" has become "salat" and "khoda hafez" has become "allah hafez." They have declared that they would tear down all the art sculptures in the country. They have routinely destroyed renderings and images of Hindu deities, Buddha, and Virgin Mary with complete impunity. Last year, they tore down many sculptures, including one of freedom fighters. And on December 5, 2020, they severely damaged a sculpture of the father of the nation, Sheikh Mujibur Rahman. This action can be equated to the tearing down, for example, of George Washington's statue or monument. We view this horrible incident as being like Mullah Omar's destruction of the two Buddha statues in Bamiyan, Afghanistan. This should be a cause for concern to the policy makers in Washington, DC.

Prime Minister Hasina is also helping the Islamists' cause by building 560 mega mosques with Saudi funding. Recently, emerging from a meeting with the Saudi Ambassador to Bangladesh in Dhaka, she declared that another eight 'iconic' mosques would be built with Saudi funding. It may be recalled that, when Saudi King was confronted by the press including Fox News accusing him of funding those mega mosques to promote the dangerous Wahabi brand of Islam. He denied it (*The Daily Star*, May 18, 2017). But the next morning, Prime Minister Hasina declared that Bangladesh itself would fund that project. By helping the Saudis promote Wahabi Islam in the country, Prime Minister Hasina is only furthering the Islamists' goal.

Barbaric Atrocities Committed By Islamists

Please recall that, between 2001 and 2005, the world witnessed a semi-Taliban situation in Bangladesh. So, it is time for the United States to ask both the Awami League and BNP to unequivocally end relationships with Jamaat-e-Islami, Hefazat-E-Islam, and all other Islamic fundamentalist and extremist groups, as has been called for by the European Union. Minorities lost their critical population mass to form a party. That is why it is impossible for minorities to run and win in any election of a democratic process. The alternative is to introduce a proportional minority quota in the parliament and the administrative process. Otherwise, minority voices and interests will be totally lost.

Also, according to different reports Bangladeshis have been facing radicalization due to other external force such as Rohingya refugees. Jamaat-e-Islami and Hefazat-e-Islam are radicalizing Rohingya children by setting up hundreds of Qawmi madrassas in the refugee camps, where there is not a single regular school for boys and girls. We know that Islamic terrorist groups' main targets for jihadists recruitment are impoverished youths like them. And as we know, al-Qaida Hind, remnants of IS and ISI, are all active in that region of Bangladesh to recruit young refugees for their cause.

Government Complicity On Atrocities

Regardless of which political party, or coalition of parties may have been in power, the vicious campaign against minorities has raged relentlessly. On the one hand, each government has discriminated against minorities in employment; denied them justice; seized their land, homes, and businesses by using a law called the Enemy Property Act (later euphemistically renamed Vested Property Act); and given their properties away to its supporters. And on the other, the Islamic nationalists, fundamentalists, and extremists have utilized various violent tactics against minorities such as blasphemy law.

Consequently, tens of millions of minorities were forced to leave the country, resulting in a sharp decline in their population. Whereas the minorities represented approximately 19 to 20 percent of Bangladesh's (then still East Pakistan's) total population in 1970, the minority population is down to less than 7 percent today. If the precedent is sustained, the minority population could be reduced to 0 percent. If violent campaign by extremists over the last few decades had not taken place, the minority population in Bangladesh today would be nearly seventy million rather than the meager twenty million that remain.[8] In Chittagong Hill Tracts, where the Indo-Mongoloid indigenous peoples represented 98 percent of the region's total population in 1947, these same people represent only 44 percent of the population today, the result of atrocities conducted against them by the Bengali Muslim settlers and security forces jointly. Based on a statistical analysis of the current rate of exodus, well-known economist Professor Abul Barakat has predicted (four years ago) that, "No Hindus will be left in Bangladesh after 30 years.[9] Two factors could play a role—exodus of minorities and unpleasant conversion".

The atrocities in Bangladesh have included the desecration and destruction of churches, temples, and deities; the burning down of dwelling houses after looting; kidnapping followed by rape and forced conversion; gang rape and mass rape; burning people alive in their homes; church massacres; and grisly murders. Tens of millions of minorities have been eliminated or driven out of the country through violence. The Awami League government has condemned this violence without any aggressive action plan or policy change. Nor has any government prosecuted and punished the perpetrators of crime against the country's religious and ethnic minorities, thus allowing the Islamists to conduct atrocities against them with complete impunity. At the directive of the high court, Prime Minister Hasina instituted a commission called the Shahabuddin Commission to investigate and submit a list of crimes perpetrated against people in the aftermath of the 2008 election. The inquiry concluded that more than 25,000 people—including 25 former ministers and MPs of the BNP-Jamaat-led alliance who are now in the opposition—related to the attacks.[10]

But Prime Minister Hasina has yet to publish the report in the

---

[8] Congressman Robert Dold, "Rep. Dold on Protecting Human Rights throughout the World," (speech on the House Floor in support of HR 440 (please listen to the Honorable Congressman at https://www.youtube.com/watch?v=IkpBiKze4Ow); S. Dastidar, *In Bangladesh: A Portrait of Covert Genocide*, 2004.

[9] Deprivation of Hindu Minority in Bangladesh: Living with Vested Property (Published English and Bengali languages 2008, 2009)

[10] BBC News, December 2, 2012.

form of a gazette or prosecute or punish the perpetrators. Some of those perpetrators could have been Sheikh Hasina's distant relatives, suggesting Bangladesh's minority lobbying case could be a foregone conclusion. The option left could be a total repatriation of all minorities to India, with a demand of compensation and proportional land from Bangladesh. In addition, it is time for Bangladesh to pursue Pakistani atrocities as genocide with the help of international bodies, including the United States of America. Biden has just declared, in 2021, the Armenian atrocities as genocide 115 years later. Similarly, Germany apologized for genocides in West Africa 113 years back.[11] Why not Bangladesh's atrocities?

The criminals are all Islamic nationalists and extremists, so the only reason the prime minister refused to prosecute and punish them is that the victims are mostly religious and ethnic minorities with no influence of considerable voter block. Clearly, when it comes to religious and ethnic minority cleansing, it is hard to distinguish among the BNP, the Jatiya Party, the Awami League, and the Islamists; *the difference is only subtle in many cases.* There is also a new trend emerging—the propagation of fake news, blasphemy rules, deepfakes, and the like. One example of a blasphemy incident was staged in 2021; a Muslim miscreant hid a Quran inside the Durga puja altar and then started rumors Hindus were degrading Islam—a subject of religious prosecution by the government.

Here are some examples of the horrendous nature of the atrocities the Islamic nationalists, fundamentalists, and extremists have conducted against the religious and ethnic minorities, with varying degrees of government complicity:

- On April 10, 1992, in the town of Logang in the Chittagong Hill Tracts, Islamists conducted a horrible massacre of the indigenous people. In a letter written to the then Prime Minister Begum Zia on November 13, 1992, seventeen US congressman, including the Honorable Nancy Pelosi, wrote, "According to reliable sources, on April 10, 1992, the town of Logang in the

---

[11] Kavena Nambira and Miriam Gleckman-Kurt, *New York Times*, July 8, 2021.

Chittagong Hill Tracts was surrounded by Bengali settlers accompanied by paramilitary forces. The inhabitants of the town were then systematically murdered. The military officials in Khagrachari admit to over 130 dead; estimates from Amnesty International and human rights organizations in Bangladesh range up to 600 or more." Thirteen more such massacres have been conducted against the indigenous peoples of Chittagong Hill Tracts alone.

- On June 3, 1997, in Baniar Char in the district of Gopalgonj, Islamists bombed a Catholic church during Sunday Mass, killing ten people and injuring twenty.

- On April 28, 1998, they destroyed and desecrated the statue of Virgin Mary and set ablaze the crucifix at St. Francis Xavier's High School in Dhaka.

- Two hundred Hindu women were mass raped by the cadres of BNP and Jamaat-e-Islami at a single spot in one night, reports *The Daily Star*, editorial page, November 16, 2001.

- During BNP rule, Jamaat-e-Islami rule (2001 to 2005), the intensity of the campaign escalated to a level that was aptly captured by the following two media headlines: "Rape and Torture Empties Villages" (*The Guardian*, July 21, 2003) and "[Bangladesh's Religious Minorities Are] Safe only in the Departure Lounge" (*The Economist*, November 29, 2003).

- On November 19, 2003, eleven members of Tejendra Sill's family were burned alive in Banskhali. Since 2012, the Islamists have continually hacked into the Facebook accounts of minorities or created fake accounts in their names. They then posted anti-Islam / anti-prophet statuses and used this as a ploy to conduct pogroms in the minority villages and neighborhoods. For example, in September 2012, in Ramu, Cox's Bazaar, twenty-five thousand Islamists rampaged through eighteen Buddhist and Hindu villages, during which they burned down homes and temples, violated women, and brutally tortured the Hindus and Buddhists. Whenever such incidents have occurred, the police have arrested the victims and incarcerated them under the Digital Security Act of 2018, rather than arresting the Islamist cybercriminals.[12] Prime Minister Hasina's courts have slapped long term-prison sentences on those innocent minority victims for "hurting the religious sentiments of the Muslims" without due process. Thus, the government the Digital Security Act is serving as the substitute for the Blasphemy Act that the Islamists have asked Prime Minister Hasina to enact. Social media is very active in Bangladesh. Strong vigilance over such activities so that it does not harm the interest of minorities is a challenge for any administration, but that must be done to avoid ongoing human tragedy.

---

[12] *"Bangladesh Enacts New Law That Could Silence Dissenters"*. *The Diplomat. Retrieved 11 May 2020 and 'Digital Security Act:A tool for harassment", Dhaka Tribune, July 2022.*

Part V

Chapter 28

Ending My Story

My story ends in this chapter, but the future story of the minority fate in Bangladesh begins here. I thought minorities had achieved long-awaited justice in Bangladesh after the liberation in 1972. Not really. It was halfway, and then all hell broke loose in 1975. India's independence from the British was a cause of celebration at its seventy-fifth anniversary in 2022. The separation of the country into two at the same time—Pakistan and India—could not be a cause of celebration. It was a day to remember for mass killings, separation of families, and the rise of Hindu-Muslim race riots. It was also the day of the forty-seventh anniversary of another separation of Pakistan into Pakistan and Bangladesh, repeating the same episode of mass killing, family separation, and a rise of minority displacement, with a similar rise in Hindu-Muslim hatred.

Six Months and Six Days is intended as a constant reminder to avoid a repetition of human tragedy. My father wanted to beat all odds—wanted not to leave the country of his birth. Like many parents, he wanted to leave his ancestral properties to his children, me included. That dream never materialized due to Hindu-Muslim tension and mass migration. We were uprooted and moved to India after his death, leaving everything in Bangladesh. I have a dream and vision now—narrated in this book. I leave it up to my two wonderful sons, Avik Chatterjee, MD, MPH, and Ayan Chatterjee, MD, MSEd, to live up to the ideals and principles for which I fought all my life. I could not leave anything else for them. I hope all human conflicts can be resolved without weapons. We need to learn the art of compromise in order to settle political, social, and even economic differences.

Chapter 29

Different Perspectives

After analyzing the history, the sufferings, and the deaths of millions, as well as the ongoing conflicts, the natural question to ask is, was the separation of India into Pakistan and India necessary? Opinions may vary. Getting independence versus separation for the sake of religion or other ethnic factors must be independently analyzed. But it may also be recognized that the past mistakes cannot be corrected by combining three countries—Bangladesh, Pakistan, and India—back to one. Generations had been brainwashed to stay separate. But human cooperation is possible with the right set of leaders and with not just political talks but also constructive and positive actions. Nine months of struggles working with multiple ethnic groups with different mindsets gave me that conviction. Of course, it will be hard work, but it's not impossible. Hindus lived under Muslim rulers for hundreds of years before the British Rule. Why not coexist independently with no hatred or animosity now? I have seen that humanity can work together when needed or life is at stake such as during the desperate revolution crisis! Joint economic, social, and educational development plan, if genuinely done, could do the same.

Many books, newspaper articles, and historical facts have been outlined by many experts before, biased or unbiased. Here, I tried to establish a different context—a new political and social environment of terrorism and hatred not highlighted, based on real and verifiable events and incidents. A good leader can make a difference. But the mindsets of those associated with the leader are also critical and important for the future. A new country can go astray due to greed, power struggles, and gullibility about a religion's rights to simply rule the land and not win the minds of its people.

When the British partitioned two countries, India and Pakistan, Hindu-Muslim tension was not felt that much—at least not in the beginning. The problem was a new country, Pakistan, was carved out of India for the sake of religion alone to please the Muslim elite. I am not sure if the isolation of the island where I grew up made a difference. Or perhaps the influence of the Islamic and military government did not filter through in the minds of the majority Muslims there. My grandparents had a lot of agricultural land. My father had three siblings; everybody's share was enough for them to live off of the land. We were on a feudal system, where farmers did all the work of growing crops with a share of 40 percent. Landowners would get 60 percent of crops because they owned the land. On the island, farmers grew our own food (staples like rice, lentils, and vegetables and fruits such as mango, pineapple, jackfruit, and coconut). In addition, fish was in abundance in the ocean, or river. The family had ponds in our backyard to grow fish as well. It was like Croatia (which I visited in 2018), where people grow olives, grapes, etc. and get fish from the coast. The islanders would buy only spices, sugar and oil imported from outside.

Furthermore, my father had the privilege and prestige of being a medical doctor. Doctors were favored and respected in our society during those periods. Dad graduated from the Calcutta Medical College with an LMF or surgery license. He got a job as a medical officer under Dunlop Plant (British Conglomerate). My grandparents forced my father to come back and practice his profession at home, so he did. They arranged a marriage for my father. My mother who was only fourteen or fifteen years old at the time of the marriage. She was from Barisal in the mainland and did not like living on the island. My doctor father ran the business side of his profession differently. Irrespective of the patients' religious or political views, he treated those who could not afford to pay the fee. And for that, he was loved. People offered him fish, vegetables, or fruits as a gift or as barter.

My mother not only did not like the island, but she also always worried for my sisters. Her worries increased after the martial law with Islamic policies was announced in 1958 as my sisters were growing up. More madrassas (Islamic religious schools) were built on the island, but there were no schools for girls. To make matters worse, Hindus were threatened as judicial panel codes were gradually changing to Islamic panel codes. While my mother worried a lot, none of these episodes sank into my head as a child, even though I was the brightest among nine brothers and sisters. Religious division and threatening did not make logical sense in my young mind. Anyhow, I was also popular at school and in my neighborhood. I studied hard. My naive goal at the time was to go to the mainland to attend a college, following in the footsteps of my older brother and to ride cars and trains. I ended up in the top forty of my high school national exam out of a million students. I qualified for a full college scholarship, a two-year program before the engineering college.

Unfortunately, my younger sister did not get the kind of opportunity I did. My mother, out of fear and hope to build a connection with India in case of total Islamization of our society, arranged an early marriage with an Indian Hindu boy. She hoped to secure a shelter in India in case she had to uproot the whole family in a moment of turmoil. This did, of course, come to fruition in 1978 after my father's death when I was in Canada. It was too late for my sisters' education.

In my childhood, religious discrimination was not remarkably visible because our minds were occupied with the nature of the island. Most smart young boys had the ambition of going to college and having a future outside Sandwip eventually. Hindu and Muslim boys played soccer and badminton together. They went to school together (including girls up to elementary level). In those younger years, Hindus had crushes on Muslims, and Muslims, on Hindus. It was an innocent, beautiful, almost perfect world. I walked two miles before I would meet a Muslim girl waiting for me outside her residence to walk together to school. Her Muslim father didn't think twice before trusting a Hindu boy like me to take his daughter to school. My Muslim classmates would invite me during the Eid festival, and we would do the same for our puja ceremony.

Muslim boys liked that Hindu girls danced and sang during the puja ceremony, which Muslim girls were rarely allowed to do.

Nonetheless, there were restrictions imposed on us by our parents. Muslim friends were free to invite Hindu friends inside their houses but Hindu boys could not. Muslim boys were not allowed inside Hindu houses. There were always those good Samaritans who wanted to change the prejudice and self-imposed segregation. One music teacher, Jogesh Chandra Banerjee, topped the list of those who wanted to break the boy-girl segregation and give girls the opportunity at high school. His unique efforts were highly appreciated. It made a huge difference in the lives of many young girls. I knew many of them being professionally successful.

I witnessed at least one full successful Hindu-Muslim romantic relationship that lasted into college. I knew it because the lovers confided in me. Today, the Hindu girl is in India and the Muslim boy in the United States.

Political propaganda scared Hindus, causing many to flee the military rule for India as Hindu-Muslim tension kicked off. Things went from bad to worse as fake rumors of communalism incidents were spread in different parts of India. The intention of the Pakistani military was to drive minorities out of the country out of hatred for Hindus and India. Almost every morning, I would hear that a Hindu acquaintance of mine had gone to India with their whole family as refugees. They were afraid to disclose their migration plans to anybody. If discovered, their daughters could be kidnapped, the family could be extorted for money, or they could be reported to the government with uncertain consequences.

When my neighbors fled to India, they would give the key to their house to a caretaker, mostly Muslims, who would occupy the house later but would tell people the landlords would return later. That never happened. My parents had difficulty explaining the phenomena to my young mind. My childhood innocence was disappearing slowly as I became college bound.

The army generals (all from West Pakistan), in collaboration with Muslim League (ML) leaders and Jamaat-e-Islam (JI), introduced the

Islamic version of the new constitution (1958) in our newly independent country called East Pakistan. The 1958 military-style constitution had many discriminatory articles, such as the Enemy Property Act. Under the new constitution, no minority could be the head of the state and so on. The worst edict was the notorious Blasphemy Laws. Military rules made it hard for Hindus to stay in East Pakistan, now Bangladesh. It was a slow but prudent realization by many minority groups as the time progressed.

The West Pakistani administration, because of its military power, was totally unfair and violated basic human rights, especially those of minorities. Unfortunately, thirty-three million West Pakistanis ruled over forty-two million East Pakistanis for over twenty-three years with unfair and whimsical attitudes. Minorities thus perceived that East Pakistan was not for minorities, especially for Hindus. That is how the Hindu population in Bangladesh was reduced to 7 percent (as of this writing in 2022) from close to 40 percent during the 1947 partition. Thus, Hindus lost a critical mass of their political and social influence in East Pakistan—contrary to the situation in India, where the Muslim population grew constantly over the years. Especially in West Bengal, the Muslim population grew to 30 percent today from 19 percent during partition. In some West Bengal districts such as Murshidabad, Maldah, Uttar Dinajpur, and others, it grew to 50 percent to 67 percent, giving the Muslim population the political and socioeconomic influence.

Backstory: Son Of A Doctor

My father wanted me to become a doctor like him. Of all my siblings, he thought I had the potential to endure the medical school. Before I could attend the university—whether for science, liberal arts, engineering, or a medical program, I first had to finish the two-year college, a two-year pre-engineering or premedical program. In the college program, I had the option to enroll in either pre-engineering, or premedical or both. I chose both options just to keep my father happy but decided to choose engineering in the end.

In 1961, I left Sandwip for my studies in college. I was always wary of what was out there beyond the sandy borders of our island. Being curious, I learned quickly about religions, politics, Indian partition, and anti-military activism. I knew real social and political education was outside the classroom. My school of choice was Victoria College in Comilla, a Hindu-dominated city. There were high schools for girls, and they could also attend the boys' college under Islamic guidelines. I always wished Mom were with me for my sisters' education.

My first political and cultural awareness in college occurred on a crisp day in February 1962 when one of my fellow students woke me up and asked me to join the Bengali language procession. By the time I was seven or eight years old, I knew of the 1952 language movement by students in Dhaka. Every year since then, students would go out with a procession in big cities. On our island, we never had a procession to remember exact date because students in high school were not that motivated for any political event. We thought only college students in big cities joined the protest. Suddenly, it dawned on me that I was now part of that city and a college student, no longer on the island or in high school. It was a wake-up call to my larger consciousness, of course.

Initially, I did not know what he was talking about. I gave him a confused look. Slowly, I started to learn the difference between the mother tongue and selecting a national language as a point of pride or heritage for official transactions. Yes, it is always a good idea to learn different languages for individual development and external communications.

Jinnah, commonly known as founding father of Pakistan, declared Urdu the only state language, though Bengalis were the majority in Pakistan. As a Bengali myself, the announcement did not sound right to me; it was announced not based on any democratic principle. Mr. Jinnah was the product of Indian democracy and the congress party. The declaration was completely unexpected, and he could have done a better job selecting a national language. It was the influence of other West Pakistani ML leaders, including the power-grabbing military, that caused the majority East Pakistani (forty-four million Bengalis out of sixty-nine million total Pakistanis) but Bengali-speaking people to be ignored. During the period of the declaration, there was a working but ineffective parliament. Jinnah never cared to raise the controversial issue in the parliament. Parliamentarians such as Dhiren Dutta, A. K. Fazlul Huq, and others though cried for a parliamentarian decision. The basic principle of commonsense democracy should have been "let the majority rule with full protection of the minority." It was totally ignored—a signal of Pakistan's sustainability.

As a nation-building effort, ignoring Bengali—the language of the majority of free Pakistan (both East and West)—was an unfair and dangerous decision that cost many lives after Jinnah's death. English as the official language would have been better given all the elites were educated and could speak English to communicate with each other. In addition, the common public could have been motivated to go to public school instead of madrassas to learn science and math and be a better workforce for the economic and industrial development of the country. Jinnah thought his charisma and name as a founding father would carry weight with Bengalis, pushing them to accept the declaration without a due democratic process. This backfired on Jinnah. Indian prime minister J. Nehru's model with majority spoken Hindi (only 30 percent) as the national language and English as the official language had worked well, and it could have worked well with Bengali/English in the East and Urdu/English in the West.

For students at universities, especially in Dhaka, political activism became routine and personal. During the four years of my university studies, I was markedly fearful of many things, including political changes that affected my life personally. First, the quota system that only 10 percent of minorities would be admitted to universities was a slap in our face. Minority students with higher scores than Muslim students could not pursue engineering or medical education simply because they were not Muslims. This did not sound right and fair. Of course, protests erupted for small reasons like this. In 1964, there was a riot regarding some holy hair stolen from the Hazratbal shrine in Kashmir, India.

Minority Hindus thousands of miles away in our part of Bangladesh had to pay the price. Some died, and some left for India. The phenomena were repeated in the 1965 war and during the 1971 liberation movement.

Family Reunion And Survival Experiences

I will never forget the moment—getting back to the normalcy of life and daily routines with my family after nine months of separation. I remained on the island with my parents for two to three days after returning to the newly freed country, Bangladesh. Amazing enthusiasm was abundant everywhere I went on the way to the island—more carefree and joyous than the anxious first month of the liberation movement. Of course, many had no idea what the next move would be? These two or three days were enough to forget the mental and emotional agonies and trauma of nine months. Love and affection from parents and relatives were powerful. I was inundated with a series of constant queries from my parents—about the escape from Kaptai, living in Barisal, and walking to the Indian border; about the people I lived with and their behavior; about my daily food and health, and so on. They wouldn't let me out of their sight for a moment.

I had similar questions for them. A heartbreaking revelation was when they described one of my friends, Fakar Ahmed, who I'd played with as a child, appearing at our door with face covered asking my mother for money and jewelry. She was initially reluctant and thought my friend was joking. In the end, my friend started beating and torturing her. Ultimately, she had to give in to their demand. I had three sisters. Traditionally, a mother starts hoarding jewelry for her daughters the day they are born and continues to do so until they are married, when she presents the jewelry as a wedding gift.

Luckily, my mother had not been killed after she'd handed over the money and jewelry. My father was, on the other hand, a confused onlooker. No help was coming from neighbors (Hindus or Muslims). Some miscreants even stole windows from the house. All good neighbors feared for their own safety first before coming to help others. Help was rare amid total lawlessness.

After the incident of an attack on my mother, some Muslim friends of my father took my family in and sheltered them for safety. That was how they survived. The family of my sister who was converted remained neutral, — maybe coming to some senses not to hurt the family further physically or emotionally during the national crisis.

It was heartbreaking to see parents' tearful eyes all day on the day of departure. They were always fearful of what could come next at my workplace.

Reintroduction of All Muslim Neighbors

All my Muslim neighbors who were supporting the West Pakistani regime were suspicious of my presence. My survival and presence on the island were a mystery to them, and they thought I would take revenge against all of them who were against the liberation or who harassed my family. Instead, I had a thought similar to the famous quote from Nelson Mandela after the liberation of South Africa, which came much later. "Reconciliation does not mean forgetting or trying to bury the pain of conflict, but that reconciliation means working together to correct the legacy of past injustice," he said in a 1995 speech.

I wanted to meet that friend who had tortured my mother and talk to him. But his whereabouts (to this day) could not be traced. I suspect he was killed by freedom fighters during the movement.

The remaining neighbors were apologetic and came to see me, wishing well. The island was peaceful for a while before the killing of Sheikh Mujibur Rahman. Islamists rose again after the assassination of Sheikh Mujibur Rahman. My Muslim brother-in-law became city mayor, running on the ML platform. My sister also played a key role in reviving the Islamism of the country.

New Work Environment

The new working environment after the liberation was another unknown to overcome. I found very few familiar faces, very few minorities, and no non-Bengalis. It was quite peaceful otherwise, with less activity. Everybody wanted to figure out their role. The good news was the army had not destroyed the dam, vital to the Bangladesh economy.

I had my own dilemma—go for high-profile job or stay low? I could have bargained for higher position in the government but decided to stay in the low-profile job for my vested interest. I was totally disappointed to see the condition of the living quarters after my return. There was a feeling of loneliness, and the work did not have the rhythm of the past. Many people were missing. My living quarters had been totally ransacked. *All* of my belongings, including official documents, clothes, and certificates, were gone. All the furniture was broken.

The reporting manager, newly hired by the Pakistani Army, stayed on the job from the beginning of the freedom struggle till we came back. It took many days to fully understand his views on the liberation. The manager welcomed all of us and was adjusting himself to the changed environment.

I cashed in my past salary for over a year and applied for leave of absence from the job. The academy functions had to be revived, and it would take months to restart. In the meantime, there was nothing much to do at the academy. My hidden reason for the leave of absence was to take care of the family and handle all the necessary logistics before going to the University of Ottawa—not an easy task. I decided to stay with friends in Dhaka, the capital of Bangladesh, and meet government officials to explain my intention of going abroad. Meanwhile, I was also trying to collect some data from other minority colleagues.

Friends Feedback As Testimony

It was an opportune time in Dhaka also to explore and collect stories of those who survived and how they survived. Everyone had a unique story. Here is a story from a classmate who lives in the United Kingdom now. Dr. Bangshi Badan Saha is a retired lecturer at West Molesey Surrey, London, UK. According to him, he is living proof of another survivor—having outrun many near-death chases. At the time of the military crackdown, he was a lecturer at the Bangladesh University of Engineering and Technology (BUET). He later went to the United Kingdom for his PhD and decided not to return to Bangladesh. Here is his personal experience narrated by him:

> 'The war or pre-war incidents—my life was endangered at least four times. The most dangerous incident occurred at the police station of a particular village called Atullah, Saturia District, Dhaka, near the Dhaleshwari River. We took shelter in a house during June and July 1971, escaping the university campus quarters, which was under the military watch. I was attacked by a Razakar with a knife. I had to run fast, as the man was coming behind me with a dagger in hand. I jumped into a canal and was able to swim across it and, thus, saved my life. The house was surrounded by water during the rainy season. Shefali, my wife, still grieves today, remembering her father, brother, and uncle were killed by Razakar at that place after my escape. Such tragic incidents traumatized my entire family life.
>
> At the time of the Pakistani military crackdown on the intellectuals of Bangladesh, on the night of March 25, 1971, I was residing at the BUET staff quarters, The military could not enter the residential compound because the entrance to the road leading to the lecturers' residence and these students' halls (near Ahsanulla Hall where we all stayed during our student life) was closed by a wall, erected by the BUET students in anticipation of the military crackdown. I could hear the gunshots during that night from my living quarters. We

learnt next that prominent Hindu lecturers of Dhaka University had been killed by the military, among them Govinda Dev, Guha Thakurta, and others. The next morning, when the curfew was lifted, I, together with three engineering students from Tangail (they were staying in my residence that night) and my young helper assistant, started leaving the city on foot. (Shefali was away for a visit to her parents' house at Mirzapur during the crackdown.) The idea was to reach Mirzapur at first.

We walked along the streets of Dhaka toward Mirpur bridge. We saw the main street was littered with dead bodies in front of Iqbal Hall, a student dorm or residence. As we walked through Iqbal Hall, we could see a big hole—made by a cannon fired by the Pakistani military at Jagannath Hall that night. The cannon hole was visible from a distance at the top of the hall.

When we came near Mirpur bridge, half a mile away from Dhaka city, we could hear gunshots. Many people formed a human chain as they were leaving the city, walking down the paddy field from the main highway and passing the bridge. We walked a total of forty miles to reach Kalikour. Then a truck driver was kind enough to give us a ride to Mirzapur.

In October, I, together with Shefali, escaped to Mankechar, Assam, India. During this journey, we stayed in a hired boat (packed with refugees) for seven days and seven nights, until we reached Assam. We faced many near-death incidents on the way to India. We were lucky to reach India alive; many were not that lucky. I can narrate many more life-threatening incidents along the way. After the liberation, I joined the department at the university and was promoted to a full professor. But I left for the United Kingdom at the earliest opportunity, and I promised to never return to Bangladesh.'

My Father's Death

My father's death was another worst nightmare for all our family members. To his credit, my father kept his promise, dying in the same place he was born and loved. We'd thought Bangladeshi freedom would bring equality, peace, prosperity, and opportunity for all. No, it was not that simple. After my father died, I, in Canada, received a frantic call from my mother, saying she could not face the injustice surrounding her due to Hindu-Muslim tension. Even our Muslim neighbors were harassing her and attempting to grab family property in my father's absence. I was compelled to advise my mother to move to India with all my younger siblings. She came to India almost penniless, and I had to support all of them from Canada.

The good "Old World" was good for my family because of my parents and grandparents. I enjoyed all the privileges of the family—a schoolteacher grandparent with vast land, a doctor father, and a loving mother. Other residents were not that lucky. Some were either killed or left the country voluntarily with their grown up children, especially girls when religious tensions rose to its highest level for many unrelated incidents. Very few could sell their properties and many left for India almost empty-handed. We as a family survived a long forty-one years (from 1947 to 1978) against all odds as minorities in a Muslim majority country with military rules. We were protected in two ways—by our isolated island and by the love of all neighbors who'd benefitted from my father's medical services. In the end, it all came crashing down.

My Family Story Of 1978

My mother died in 1997 in Kolkata, India. Our properties remain in Bangladesh, occupied by Muslim neighbors, though some of them did not have any choice due to erosion of their homes by the sea. What happened to my family did not match the feeling I'd had about our island during my childhood, when the village needed my father's help during cholera epidemics or after cyclones and tidal waves hit the island. I remember the day in 1961 when a cyclone trapped my father and I in bed when the roof collapsed and neighbors rescued us. Right after the rescue, my father provided medical help to cyclone-affected victims. My father was blind and never saw the dark side of the society's evolution. It was very unlike my father when he warned me not to visit him on his deathbed in 1978.

Displaced people uprooted from their centuries old ancestral home have an emotional feeling that never goes away. Turning that feeling into a constructive vision is a human achievement—one I always aspired to. In all my stay abroad, I felt so sad for the people I left behind. Those people deserved better from the Bangladesh administration but were disappointed. I, myself, feel depressed and frustrated. I'm convinced that writing 'Six Months and Six Days' to create an impact on the future generation is the only remedy. I know I cannot get consensus through the book, but even for a few, it may do the trick. Social changes always occur due to the efforts of a few thinkers and philosophers among a society.

If all attempts to bring about social fairness and justice fail, the only choice is to demand a total repatriation of all minorities from Bangladesh to India, with an arrangement of proportional land from the Bangladeshi government. Yes, some Bangladeshi expatriates are well positioned to raise some favorable terms with the Indian government while sending money to relatives in India. More foreign exchange from the Bangladeshi diaspora could flow to India if the Indian government were to relax regulations on opening bank accounts, acquiring properties, or starting businesses for relatives. The accumulated sum of such transactions would be in terms of billions of dollars for Indian foreign exchange per year.

Internal Conflicts In Party (AL)

The united and well-coordinated Awami League during the liberation started falling apart after independence. It was split into two. One faction was the insurgent left-wing party, called Gonobahini, and the other, a government-managed party called Jatiya Rakhi Bahini, was formed to counter it. Unfortunately, there was so much killing between these two parties, especially in major cities that it was, again, scary to talk of a third party by minorities. Fair and honest elections were not possible in such a chaotic scene. All minority candidates were always vulnerable to harsh criticism of conspiracy by all other majority parties. There was widespread fear of economic downfall and famine.

Fortunately, Bangladesh recovered from the 1971 economic downfall well, with a good year in 1972 of staple food production and foreign aid from different countries. Sheikh Mujibur Rahman selected his cabinets before the constitution was framed for the general election. He did it twice within a month from his transition of presidency to prime minister ship. Only one cabinet minister, Mr. Phani Bhushan Majumder, was selected from the minority group. It was a token selection compared to the sacrifice by different minority groups during the movement. The minority group was so diminished—in power, scope, and capability—that there was hardly any chance to compete in the general election.

The theory of stable government is based on elected representatives from multiple diverse parties with broad, diverse ideological, social, and political backgrounds. No chance was given to such principles, and power grabs by one party soon dominated the field. Khondaker Mostaq Ahmed, minister of power, started the trouble. He was a controversial AL leader even during the period when the Bangladesh government was in exile. He was in India but wanted a peaceful negotiation with Pakistan. Rumor had it he was even behind the conspiracy to assassinate Mujibur Rahman. He became temporary president of Bangladesh by replacing a Mujib loyalist. Army Chief Ziaur Rahman took over the administration by an army coup from Mostaq's loyalists.

Serious Footnotes For Government's Attention

In my mind, it was too a short time to transform the Bangladesh sociopolitical infrastructure. The Pakistani mindset had dominated the Bangladeshi mindset for many decades, and it was not easy to make that paradigm change. Nine months of struggle showed a small window of what could have been done, but more sustainable transformation was needed by strong leadership, which was missing after Sheikh Mujibur Rahman's death. This is not only my view. Many experts, political researchers, scholars, and historians think similarly. The Bangladeshi diaspora living abroad is over several million and economically solvent. They are very active outside the country and have accumulated many issues and grievances to be seriously looked at and corrected. Discussions within the country have become impossible because of the social and political atmosphere and personal hatred and attack by majority parties.

Let us cite some issues and immediate remedies based on the reality on the ground that exists today. Solutions must be congenial to the minority community (this accumulated list may not be necessarily exhaustive):

- No international relationship could last long without Pakistan's full apology and financial compensation for displaced families.
- In 1971, by partnering with the Pakistan Army, Islamists conducted an atrocity in which three million unarmed progressive Muslims, minority Hindus, Buddhists, and Christians were butchered; two hundred thousand women were raped; and nearly ten million were forced to flee the country. It is time for the international bodies to acknowledge the atrocities as genocide.
- After the assassination of the founding father, Sheikh Mujibur Rahman, another episode of violence against minorities by the Islamist government erupted, and many lives were disrupted. But nobody was held accountable. Correct census data is not yet available, but it is a large number. Repeat of such episodes has become routine and must be stopped.
- On April 30, 1992, Harkat-ul-Jihad-al-Islami Bangladesh (HuJI-B), which was then training jihadists in several camps in Bangladesh, demanded that Bangladesh be converted into an

Islamic state.[13] Religious parties, along with religious campaigns to demean minorities should be banned, as in the original constitution.

- Harkat-ul-Jihad-al-Islami Bangladesh's chief Fazlur Rehman Khalil, one of the six signatories on Osama bin Laden's 1998 Declaration of Holy War against the United States is roaming free.[14] The United States needs to be vigilant to avoid sheltering any religious extremists in Bangladesh.

- By 2000, the Islamists exported jihadists to fight for the Taliban government in Afghanistan, alongside Bin Laden's Al-Qaeda.[15] In his interview with CNN reporters, Mr. Pelton and John Lindh reported that the "Ansar al Islam is composed of different branches according to ethnic groups. The language is divided into Bengali, Urdu, and Arabic." Such international transportation of terrorists for religious fight should not be allowed by Bangladesh.

- Around 2001, the Islamists of Bangladesh declared their goal of creating a larger, more monolithic Islamic state in Bangladesh by annexing the Arakan province of Burma and parts of the neighboring Indian states.[16] This has been consistently reiterated by every Islamist group operating in Bangladesh. The issue must be carefully investigated, and perpetrators of crimes must be punished.

- It was at that time that there were slogans in Dhaka like, "Amra sobai hobo Taliban, Bangla hobe Afghanistan" (We shall all be Taliban, and Bangladesh will be another Afghanistan).[17] It's a very sad episode to be reckoned with.

---

[13] Bertil   Lintner,   https://www.satp.org/satporgtp/countries/bangladesh/terroristoutfits/huj.htm.

[14] *Los Angeles Times*, July 2, 2008.

[15] CNN.com/WORLD, December 21, 2001.

[16] *Time* (online edition), October 14, 2002.

[17] Eliza Griswold, "The Next Islamist Revolution," *The New York Times Magazine*, January 23, 2005.

- After the fall of Afghanistan, not only did the Bangladeshi jihadists return to Bangladesh, there also came a shipload of foreign Afghan war veterans as reported by M. V. Mecca.[18] Jamaat-e-Islami engaged these war veteran jihadists as trainers in the Qawmi madrassas and various camps in the mountains of Chittagong Hill Tracts—an episode to be banned.

- In October 2001, Jamaat-e-Islami and its allies ascended to power by partnering with the Islamic nationalist party of BNP and unleashed a reign of terror in the country, which forced tens of thousands of minorities to leave the country in masse.[19] In addition, many progressive Muslims were forced to seek refuge abroad—stop ongoing saga like this.

- By that time, the Islamic extremists of Bangladesh became so powerful that we frequently saw such media headlines as "Beware of Bangladesh" and "Bangladesh: A Cocoon of Terror"[20] or "In Bangladesh, as in Pakistan, a Worrisome Rise in Islamic Extremism."[21] Regulate extremism.

- In 2004, the Islamists conducted a grenade attack on the current prime minister's meeting in which twenty-four political leaders and supporters were killed and three hundred were injured. The prime minister narrowly survived. Should it be the fate of future progressive leaders?

- In 2005, Islamic extremists simultaneously exploded five hundred bombs in three hundred locations throughout the country in a show of strength. Stop all such possibilities.

- In 2013, with the support of BNP, Hefazat-e-Islam and Jamaat-e-Islami, Islamists marched to Dhaka with hundreds of thousands of their cadres and allies and seized the city in an attempt to overthrow Sheikh Hasina's government and establish

---

[18] Alex Perry, "Deadly Cargo."
[19] *The Guardian*, July 21, 2003.
[20] *Far Eastern Economic Review*, April 4, 2002.
[21] *The Wall Street Journal*, April 2, 2002.

a caliphate in Bangladesh.[22] Bangladesh constitution should not accommodate such platform.

- In recent years, Islamists have killed many intellectuals, journalists, foreign clergy members, NGO personnel, bloggers, and educators, including foreigners—tough vigilance required.

- In 2016, Bangladeshi jihadists affiliated with IS conducted the Holey Artisan Bakery Café massacre, during which they uploaded dead bodies on social media as they slaughtered them, in IS style.[23] Such thought must be discouraged.

- Most recently, Hefazat-E-Islam's Ameer has demanded that the Hindus and the Ahmadiyya Muslims be declared *kafirs* (infidels).[24] Hefazat-E-Islam has also declared that they will pull down all the statues in the country, including that of the father of the nation, Sheikh Mujibur Rahman, citing that it is against sharia.[25] That is why revival of the original constitution is required.

- Recently, the Islamists have declared that they will tear down all the statues and sculptures in the country, and on December 5, 2020, they vandalized a statue of the Sheikh Mujibur Rahman— what a pity not to punish such behavior?

These are all examples of minority marginalization in Bangladesh by extremist operators. The author believes that saving the minorities of Bangladesh is a moral and strategic obligation on the part of the United States and Bangladesh. Several immediate policy changes are in order:

- Enact a hate speech and hate crime law and prosecute and punish the perpetrators of crimes against the country's minorities in a special tribunal under that law, starting by making the list of criminals available in the Sahabuddin Commission Report.

---

[22] *The Daily Star*, April 7, 2013.
[23] BBC NEWS, July 2, 2016; Reuters, December 1, 2016.
[24] *Dhaka Tribune*, February 13, 2019.
[25] BDNews24.com, November 28, 2020.

- Provide reparations to the victims of persecution for their loss of life and property and help them with the rehabilitation process. Revisit the Enemy Property Repeal Act (aka Vested Property Law) to include provision for the owners and their heirs' right to claim property that was seized under the Enemy Property Act, regardless of their current residency status, as in Germany or Turkey, and then implement it quickly.
- Reinstate non-Muslim writers in the textbooks. Remove the section in the fifth grade Islamiat in which non-Muslims have been denied the status of humans and likened to animals. Regulate the so-called "interpretation of religion in mammoth gatherings" so that the clerics may no longer dehumanize non-Muslims, spread hatred, or encourage Muslims to attacks minorities and seize their property.
- Employ minorities in the spirit of affirmative action in positions of powers and prestige, including the security forces, armed forces, foreign service, and so on.
- Restore indigenous peoples' right to refer to themselves as Adivasis people, since they were the first humans to inhabit the region, where they have lived for centuries.

Being Vigilant On Minority Concerns

I thought fighting for Bangladeshi minority rights during the Pakistani regime to restore the dignity of humanity was a worthy cause. Unfortunately, Bangladesh did not protect its minorities' rights other than for a short period, from 1972 to 1975. Minority rights were shattered by the assassination of Sheikh Mujibur Rahman and the Islamization of the constitution. So, the fight for minorities cannot stop now. I am not in the country, and that gives me extra leverage of influence via international politics. Reversal of the fair and nonreligious constitution with minority rights started with Major Ziaur Rahman in 1975. Major Zia was the first high-ranking officer of the Pakistan

Army to defect and declare Bangladeshi independence. The Islamization reached its climax during the presidency of Hussain Muhammad Ershad and then Khaleda Zia (wife of major Ziaur Rahman). Efforts have been undertaken in Bangladesh, the United States, and Canada by many minority Bangladeshis like me to restore confidence in the country for all—majority and minority.

With the liberation of Bangladesh from Pakistan, some causes of the civil war were eliminated but not all. There were many causes of the Bangladeshi civil war. Six are cited here:

1. Language and culture differences
2. Desire for Muslims only country and a reincarnation of the Ottoman Empire
3. Military dictatorship and the undermining of a huge minority population
4. Political and religious discrimination
5. Economic exploitation of East Pakistan (now Bangladesh) by West Pakistan
6. Influence of foreign powers, especially Islamic countries
7. Gullibility of Bangladeshi leaders when it came to the influence and interests of foreign leaders.

Instead of working toward the harmonious coexistence of all people, Muslim League and military leaders aggressively promoted Islamic causes for their own benefits from day one in 1947 when Pakistan was partitioned. Dissatisfaction was fermenting, and it reached its climax on March 25, 1971. I feel items one and five have been eliminated by the liberation of Bangladesh. The others should be analyzed carefully for the future stability of Bangladesh. Pakistani power being out of the picture, other new and similar events manipulated by Bangladeshi leaders are of concerns for the stability and well-being of minorities.

The founding father was assassinated. The constitution was manipulated and compromised. The original Pakistani supporters not fighting for the liberation are being very vocal in Bangladesh. Minorities who fought and sacrificed the most, are being threatened and harassed.

The displacement of my own family in 1978 was one such example. The Rohingya problem has complicated regional politics. The GDP growth is encouraging. The rise of radical Islamization and the attitude of Bangladesh toward India are not improving. Each of these elements will have their share in contributing to the trajectory of future Bangladesh. Stability of the country may be under question if the current state of affairs continues after the defeat of the current prime minister, Sheikh Hasina. I focus on these because their potential impact on minority communities.

The political and economic fights between China and the United States are reminiscent of the cold war between the USSR and the United States after World War II, which existed for decades. China has ignited a cold war with the United States in the South Asian region, and its outcome could be detrimental to world peace. Bangladesh may be a willing or forced participant in the Russia-China axis opposing the US-India axis. It shows a return to the difficulties of the cold war political climate that existed after World War II with more players involved now - China, Pakistan, Russia, India, and Bangladesh. Sliding of N. Modi in Putin's orbit to contain India-China tension as reported in Yahoo news, May 1, 2023.

Given all these, Bangladeshi Minorities urge the US government and lawmakers to act now—not only to save Bangladesh's remaining twenty million religious and ethnic minorities but also to firmly establish a secular/humanistic democracy there. Echoing what Selig Harrison wrote in the *Los Angeles Times*, July 2008, we want to say, "Get a grip on Dhaka," and do not write off democracy in Bangladesh yet. The Islamists of Bangladesh must not be allowed to hold the entire country hostage. The issue can be addressed by the global community of secular democratic nations; these goals can still be achieved without military intervention. We urge you to act now, before Bangladesh becomes a failed state. Bangladesh shows all symptoms of Pakistan to fail—anti-India sentiments, anti-minority sentiments, radical Islamism, and government complicity. I, like many other activists, hoped Bangladesh would be a model Islamic democratic country in the world. Oh God, were we deeply wrong! Opportunists benefitted, but real fighters or patriots were disappointed. Let us recap what we achieved, what is yet to achieve, and how we can do so. Unfortunately, the job is not yet half complete. And ongoing struggles, nationally and internationally by the minority, are rising due to indifference by the government in power.

Memory of February 21

Eventually, February 21 became a part of the International Language Day many decades after the original movement and sacrifice. Yes, we addressed language, culture, and economic exploitation by West Pakistan. The photo included here shows the symbol of pride for the Bengali language movement—Shaheed Minar, built in memory of the martyrs of the language movement, killed by West Pakistani forces starting in February 1952. The initial protest started at Dhaka University after Mr. Jinnah's declaration of Urdu as the only state language. Then it became a national protest, spreading all over East Pakistan year after year. Many students lost their lives since then. Slowly, the students' demand was eventually linked with political demands. Ultimately, UNESCO recognized the language movement and declared February 21 the International Mother Language Day. This was the day when students died protesting Jinnah's declaration of Urdu to be the state language. Since then, Bangladesh got the authority to promote the Bengali language and culture internationally.

Shaheed Minar of The Bengali Language Movement
As Displayed On The Annual Anniversary.

Release of Mujibur Rahman

During the liberation movement, the whereabouts of Mujibur Rahman, commonly known as Banga Bandhu (friend of Bengalis), was not fully disclosed to the general population—it was unclear whether he was dead, alive, or jailed. The Pakistan Army intentionally kept that information secret so his supporters would not be motivated to fight the army. That angered the population, and they became ready to fight, even with homemade tools. After the liberation, Pakistan faced international pressure to release Mujibur Rahman. Mujibur Rahman returned to Bangladesh on January 10, 1972, via two short stops, one in London, UK, and another in Delhi, India.

Z. A. Bhutto tried to play another trick with Mujib here as well. Bhutto told Mr. Rahman before the release that he was alive because of Mr. Bhutto. In other words, Mr. Bhutto saved Mujib's life from army prosecution; this was a false pretense, though. Knowing Mr. Bhutto's character, Mr. Rahman did not pay any attention to his whispered claim. Moreover, it was too late—after so many deaths and so much destruction. Pakistan did not maintain any scope of reconciliation. Bhutto was hopeful of a good future liaison with Bangladesh against India, again taking the plea of Islamization. Bhutto even boasted of a statement from Yahya Khan saying, "It was a blunder not killing Mujib."

I was not in Dhaka but watched it on different TV channels, including the BBC and Akashvani Kolkata. Mujib was given a warm welcome by people, and Mujib, in his speech, expressed his gratitude to India and congratulated the Bangladeshis who fought for a country at the same Dhaka racecourse where it all started on March 1971 before army crackdowns. He reiterated his four principles of Bangladesh's new constitution, nationalism, secularism, democracy and socialism. I was feeling so good inside and murmured to myself that we as minorities had gotten what we wanted after forty-five years of oppression.

Mujib faced many unprecedented challenges—no money in the reserved bank, the farmers' inability to grow any crops for a year or so, and the rise of corruptions that led to a famine in 1974. Many adverse circumstances could have been attributed to West Pakistani business ownership in East Pakistan. West Pakistani business enterprises sent their money to West Pakistan. They even robbed common people of their private cars and other mobile resources on the street and shipped them to West Pakistan before the last day of the military surrender to freedom fighters. Bangladesh's reserve bank did not have any money to operate. A note here. Mr. Bhutto, in the end, received his punishment—prosecution and then death in 1979 by the military after another coup by the Pakistan Army General, Mohammad Zia-ul-Huq.

New Country With Unprecedent Feeling

The freedom in a short period beyond perceived belief gave all Bangladeshis a surprise and invigorating feeling never seen before. The contrasting scenario before and after the movement revealed the real human character. This period was very revealing for me—I saw greed versus life's ambition. Of course, there were many chaotic situations within the new government. After the initial emotional outburst with my parents in the island, I took my journey back to my workplace at Kaptai Academy, Chittagong Hill Tract district. I could have lobbied for a higher position in the new Bangladesh administration but decided to stay in the low-profile job to complete the logistics of going abroad. I also had a gut feeling that the Islamization that had gripped two generations of the majority East Pakistanis, ingrained by the Pakistani military might not change overnight.

Let me highlight my experience through some short stories. Overall, was a bag of mixed emotion for all. There was joy for the freedom fighters and confusion for the military supporters and Islamists. Nepotism and favoritism reached the top level of the administration. The political power struggle of the early administration was unthinkable when those who weren't freedom fighters made unreasonable demands for a higher share. As an independent country, Bangladesh had created opportunities that could not be imagined during the Pakistani regime for many. India government's attitude of indifference, coupled with Indian businesses' profit-mongering business transactions were not helping either. There was rivalry among different groups all trying to get a favor from the founding father, Sheikh Mujibur Rahman, a good activism organizer but with little experience of running a government administration. Spontaneous and whimsical decisions by the founding father were confusing at best. Moreover, civil administrators who remained loyal to the West Pakistani regime could not be trusted who was controlling the administration.

These months of chaos told me enough to see that Bangladesh could be heading for another disaster, and that was what my minority friends and I discussed among ourselves. We saw the Muslim character in Pakistan's history, and that was what was happening in 1975 and afterward, after the assassination of the founding father. The difference was it was Bengali Muslims, not the non-Bengali Muslims of West Pakistan. Those Bengalis who were Pakistani supporters in high positions were pardoned by the founding father. It was a strategic blunder, but there was no other choice to get the country back on track of a free country logistically.

Indira Gandhi's Historic Visit To Bangladesh

A visit by a foreign leader like Indira Gandhi was unprecedented in the twenty-three-year history of the then East Pakistan—unbelievable vibe and joy never seen before. People chanted, "Joy Bangla" (a slogan during the liberation movement) in their loudest voices possible. Her visit marked a historic signing of an agreement between Bangladesh and India. Words simply cannot describe the scene of people's jubilance during her entire visit. Bangladeshis lined up to see a glimpse of her face along the airport road or any other place she visited. People were glued to TV sets at homes, business, and clubs and, in fact, wherever they could get one. Indira Gandhi's first and last visit to Bangladesh occurred on March 17, 1972. Bangladeshis saluted her for her role during the nine-month liberation movement. Her role can be characterized as a brilliant diplomatic and strategic maneuver of the world's opinion against a powerful nation like the United States. The step-by-step process she followed was meticulous, which many of us perceived in the fighting trenches. Many strategies worked in her favor against many odds, among them:

- Providing moral support to Bangladeshi fighters starting from March 27, 1971
- Hosting refugees crossing the border to avoid Pakistan Army atrocities
- Housing the provisional Bangladesh government in exile in India
- Training freedom fighters in war logistics for sustainability
- Mobilizing international support from countries such as the USSR and Canada
- Declaring war when Pakistan started a preemptive air strike on December 3, 1971
- Almost unconditional release of ninety thousand Pakistani soldiers with a hope for a long-term peace accord with Pakistan (which Pakistan never followed through because of inherent hatred to India and Indians)

In the trip, both leaders signed a treaty of peace and cooperation between the two countries for twenty-five years. Unfortunately, there were twelve articles of understanding in the treaty. None of the leaders could see the results of their long efforts because both leaders were assassinated; Mujib in 1975 and Gandhi in 1984. After the death of Mujib, the history of Bangladesh was distorted by the Islamists. The Bangladeshi military and Islamists dominated the administration of Bangladesh from 1975 to 2008, almost repeating the episode of the Pakistani military. Indira Gandhi and many other Indian heroes did not even receive the honor they deserved for their sacrifice on behalf of Bangladesh during these years.

Finally, when Sheikh Hasina came into power through a democratic process, she acknowledged the dedication of Indira Gandhi and rewarded her with the highest foreign award, the Bangladesh Swadhinata

Sammanona (Bangladesh Freedom Honor). Sheikh Hasina also awarded many other honors to other Indians (civilians and army personnel) for their work—a noble gesture, of course, which was ignored by the previous three administrations for a long time. Many goals and promises are yet to be fulfilled.

Revival Of The 1972 Constitution

The ideal constitution was almost in place. It lost its way due to a military coup in 1975. Millions fought to liberate the country and for a number of causes reflected in the original framework of the Bangladesh constitution. These included democracy based on equal voting rights, no campaigns based on religion, and no discriminatory or religious regulations. Unfortunately, Bangladeshis faced the same fate from 1975 to 2008 as East Pakistanis had faced during the military rule, from 1952 to 1970. I hope it does not take another revolution to get the original 1972 constitution installed.

Pakistan's Apology

It is time for the world to know that Pakistan did not protect its minorities— Hindu, Christian, Buddhist, and other. Pakistan was supposed to make an official apology before any relationship could be restored with Bangladesh. Pakistan was also supposed to punish some of the ninety thousand military leaders captured during the surrender. This never materialized because of the changed values of Bangladeshi politics and government and Islamic politics in the subcontinent. Bangladesh must correct its course now for the sake of its minorities and its displaced people. Such people deserve compensation from Pakistan in order to be rehabilitated. It is never too late, though close to fifty years of history has since passed.

Declaration Of Pakistan's Atrocities As Genocide

International bodies, due to the influence of the United States, kept silent on the Bangladeshi atrocities. The United States was one of the last few countries to recognize Bangladesh after Bangladesh became a chartered member of the UN. No action has yet been taken to declare the killing of three million Bengalis (the majority being Hindus) as a genocide by Pakistan. Such genocide can be compared with the Holocaust massacres. President Biden has taken a good stand after over a hundred years against the Ottoman Empire, declaring the killing of 1.5 million Armenians a genocide[26]. Germany did the same declaration of its atrocity in Namibia after 113 years. A declaration of genocide in 1971 by international bodies would bring some justice for Bangladeshis and accountability to Pakistan, even if it has been fifty years—a step that is historically not unprecedented. It is time for the world to know that Pakistan did not protect its minorities, Hindu, Christian, Buddhist, and other. Pakistan must face some accountability as an exemplary punishment for the sake of a regional peaceful coexistence. Many thanks to Congressman Ro Khanna and ex-congressman Steve Chabot for their house resolution 1430 of October 14, 2022, It is time for the whole house to vote on it and approve it for the President Biden to sign it – a just cause to avoid further deterioration of humanity.

Recommendations With Pros And Cons

All recommendations are apparently tall and short. Only the current prime minister, Sheikh Hasina, can make a difference. She may be the last survivor of her family who faced Pakistan's ongoing torture for over twenty-three years and more under the Bangladesh military. Past circumstances also allowed her to develop some empathy for minorities. Her actions are sometimes confusing under current circumstances, due to Islamic influence, though. After her departure, the future could look

---

[26] 'Breaking with Predecessors, Biden Declares Mass killings of Armenians a Genocide' by Katie Rogers and Carlotta Gall, NYT, April 24, 2021.

bleaker. I make this plea because our struggles beyond the language movement have remained unfulfilled since the liberation because of the ongoing Islamization of the country. Two generations that grew after the liberation could not realize what they got because history was altered, including the change in the constitution. Gaps between our dream and vision and the reality on the ground were increased due to the Bangladeshi military coup, the influence of radical Islam, the killing of the founding father, and the remnant of many Pakistani-style discriminatory government policies and regulations toward minorities.

I left Bangladesh in 1972 to pursue higher studies in Canada, hoping for a real secular and democratic Bangladesh after twenty-four years of oppressive military rule (from 1947 in 1971) in Pakistan. But my dream and the dreams of other minorities were shattered. The success and the expected trajectory of Bangladesh becoming a secular and progressive country did not last long. The founding father, Sheikh Mujibur Rahman, was assassinated, and all hopes of minorities came to a halt for the next thirty-three years (from 1975 to 2008). Bangladeshi minorities faced similar traps of discrimination that existed in Pakistan.

The players, this time, were different; the Bangladesh military who had been previously trained in Pakistan. This is another reason to document my experience—the doubling down of the pain. During this period, there was another mass exodus of minorities (mostly Hindus) to India, including my family. That reduced the minority population to less than eight percent in Bangladesh, with a trend of a continuous decline.[27] The unofficial number of Hindus in Bangladesh may be less than 5 percent now.

The future does not look good either—which is the main theme of the book. Why this view? The prime minister, Sheikh Hasina, is under the pressure of Islamization. The constitution changes by Islamist rulers from 1978 onward are another such example. To stay in power via democracy, she needs to win over the right-wing conservatives during

---

[27] TBS Report, July, 27, 2022, last modified July, 27, 2022.

election - a tall political manipulation[28]. Can the political manipulation be normalized for a true democracy? Her strong leadership aligning with international maneuvering power over disgraced political parties may restore true democracy people sacrificed for. I feel optimistic with skepticism during Hasina's regime but pessimistic after her departure from the premiership. There are three emphatic or obligatory reasons: (1) She survived the family assassination. (2) She lived in India during the liberation movement or during Bangladeshi military coup (3) India assisted to mobilize progressive forces in Bangladesh for her election win in 2008. She brought much normalizations of the country after 1975 to 2008 turmoil, but fear of return of extremism in the future is certain after Hasina's departure given the current political climate. There is a strong possibility even now of a return to Bangladesh-India tension as it existed during the Pakistan-India tension before 1971. Hasina has a responsibility to diffuse this tension for generations to come, and it would also be prudent for her to improve the situation for the future peace of that region. She is in a unique position as well because of her personal family tragedy. The new administration after her would have a tougher task because of the Islamization of the country. No other Muslim leader would ever have any empathy for minorities, as we observed from 1975 to 2008 or even now. Unfortunately, very few changes or modifications in the constitution since 1978 have been reversed during Sheikh Hasina's parliamentarian administration.

While building my life in Canada, I worried constantly about the well-being of family, relatives, and friends in Bangladesh under the changed environment. The situation was so bad after Mujib's death that my father warned me not to visit Bangladesh. My life could have been in danger. My father, like many other fathers, wanted to leave something behind (tradition or wealth) for his children and grandchildren. My father repented of his failure at the end of his life for reasons beyond his control (human created). This book is my attempt to leave behind

---

[28] Origins and Pitfalls of Confrontational Politics in Bangladesh by Muhammad Mustafizur Rahaman, South Asian Survey and Does Bangladesh's PM still believe in democracy? By Nahal Toosi, Alexander Ward, and Lawrence Ukenye, Politico.

something for my children and grandchildren – a promise of holding human civilization and high ideals of humanity above all.

I say enough is enough. Let me take a hard look and suggest some appropriate alternative suggestions and may be actions. Based on incidents highlighting what Bangladesh's Islamists represent politically and the barbaric atrocities they have perpetrated, I came up with different options and rationales in case the Bangladesh government fails to make a full restoration of the 1972 constitution and Hindu-Muslim-Christian-Buddhist harmony. Some may think they might not be realistic or practical or may consider them extreme for leaders to consider. Yes, the fight for the liberation of Bangladesh was also extreme.

The Possibility of A Minority Party

The platform of the existing party system is not conforming to minority interests. In each party's manifesto, Islam is always highlighted. Formation of a minority party is a democratic and logical step. There was a possibility of forming the coalition of all minorities along with some majority factions. For the success of such a party, a politically motivated critical minority mass with resources would be required. In addition, the process must have the majority support for infrastructure and sustainability. Problems are (1) there is no critical mass to form such a party; (2) minorities do not have the mindset, high moral and resources under the current environment; and moreover, (3) polarization among ethnic groups has reached its climax, making negotiated compromise a no-go without outside interference by a neutral organization such as the UN or the International Criminal Court (ICC). Otherwise, leaders of said minority party would be targeted by radical Islamists. Indications of the brutal attitude of killing by radical groups have been cited in abundance.

Proportional Representation Of Minorities

Minorities are hardly represented in the current parliament, and day-to-day minority issues are ignored or decided in an arbitrary way. That is not a good sign that a country will prosper. Minority groups will become slowly disenfranchised. Two options are possible to correct the situation. For one, a leading member of the minority group by rotation may be selected at the cabinet level to have a view when government policies are developed. The other option to select proportional representation of the minority from every community to the parliament. The job of these representatives would be to ensure a democratic process in terms of policy making decisions—not the benevolence of the majority. Leaving complex socioeconomic issues up to the majority not only cannot serve the nation well but is also leading to a situation where minorities are becoming a quickly disappearing species. This is not a fully democratic process but is an option when the majority rules to ensure full protections of minority interests.

Alternatively, new voting districts only for minorities based on the concentration of the minority population may be defined for a proportional representation. Equal rights voter policies in the United States may be a good example to follow[29].

Reparation of Minorities – An Ultimatum

Returns of lands and properties of minorities are a reasonable demand given all options fail. Over the history of Pakistan, minorities abandoned their properties in Bangladesh and took refuge in India to save their lives—an ultimatum overdue for a fair settlement now and in future. This drastic course would be one to take only after all other options have failed. Bangladesh took a dramatic turn three years after liberation, unexpectedly. The fate of minorities fell to the same level as had befallen them during Pakistani rule. The Bangladeshis, or the country's minorities, alone cannot improve the situation. Bangladesh and its people do not have the necessary international political clout and cannot do much without outside influence because of its lack of resources for seeking justice.

This is not an unprecedented example. A similar situation happened during the partition of India and Pakistan between East and West

---

[29] 'Voting Rights: A Short History' By Carnegie Corporation of New York, November 18 2019.

Punjab. Similarly, if Bangladesh is indifferent, India can take back control of all minorities with a demand of proportional land from Bangladesh. More than two million Bangladeshis are living abroad permanently in different countries. I presume close to 30 percent may be from different minority groups. Two such minority groups are very active in the United States. They are the Human Rights Congress for Bangladesh minority (HRCBM) and Bangladesh Hindu Buddhist Christian Unity Council (BHBCUC). All members of those groups are willing to send a large sum of foreign funds to India if the Indian government takes constructive actions. In fact, the process is already in place unofficially. Like me, many have supported repatriation of their relatives and families to India. It is a question of the Indian government legitimizing the process for the sake of humanity. A negotiation of this radical view with Bangladesh would be effective when a proper levy is placed for the land for minorities.

This is an extreme view, I understand. It could also lead to another fight involving the territorial separation of a country. Fights for territory always cause killings, family separation, and hatred among ethnic groups. We have seen it after India and Pakistan in 1947 and then Pakistan and Bangladesh in 1971. Hopefully, such lessons will convince thoughtful leaders to be cautious in their actions. Preserving humanity, peace, and race relations should be a priority. Can this be a wish after my death when all fails? Unless a country with a territory manages religious extremism and its associated power the human civilization may suffer in the end.

Abbreviations

AL	Awami League
AWRF	Arab War Relief Fund
BBC	British Broadcasting Corporations
BHBCUC	Bangladesh Hindu, Buddhist, Christian Unity Council
BNP	Bangladesh Nationalist Party
BSTI	Board Of Science, Technology and Innovation
BUET	Bangladesh University of Engineering and Technology
CBI	Central Bureau of Investigation
CIB	Central Intelligence Branch
DSW	Director of Students Welfare
EPSU	East Pakistan Students Union
HRCBM	Human Rights Congress For Bangladesh Minority
IAF	Indian Air Force
IAS	Indian Administrative Service
ICC	International Criminal Court
INA	Indian National Army
IS	Islamic State
ISI	Islamic State of Iraq
LOC	Line Of Control
MB	Measurement Book
NAP	National Awami Party
NCAFA	North Carolina Agriculture Finance Authority
PAF	Pakistan Air Force
PPP	Pakistan People's Party
UN	United Nation

UNESCO	United Nations Educational Scientific and Cultural Organization
VIP	Very Important Person
VP	Vice President
WAPDA	Water And Power Development Authority

Printed in the United States
by Baker & Taylor Publisher Services